D0160361

Edgar Allan Poe

OTHER BOOKS BY PAUL COLLINS

Banvard's Folly: Thirteen Tales of People Who Didn't Change the World

Sixpence House: Lost in a Town of Books

Not Even Wrong: A Father's Journey into the Lost History of Autism

*The Trouble With Tom: The Strange Afterlife and Times of
    Thomas Paine*

The Book of William: How Shakespeare's First Folio Conquered the World

*The Murder of the Century: The Gilded Age Crime That Scandalized
    a City & Sparked the Tabloid Wars*

*Duel With the Devil: The True Story of How Alexander Hamilton &
    Aaron Burr Teamed Up to Take On America's First Sensational
    Murder Mystery*

Edgar Allan Poe

THE FEVER CALLED LIVING

PAUL COLLINS

ICONS SERIES

New Harvest
Houghton Mifflin Harcourt
BOSTON . NEW YORK
2014

This edition published by special arrangement with Amazon Publishing

For information about permission to reproduce selections from this book,
go to www.apub.com.

www.hmhco.com

Library of Congress Cataloging-in-Publication Data
Collins, Paul, date.
Edgar Allan Poe : the fever called living / Paul Collins.
pages cm
Includes bibliographical references and index.
ISBN 978-0-544-26187-7
1. Poe, Edgar Allan, 1809–1849.   2. Authors, American —
19th century — Biography.   I. Title.
PS2631.C65 2014
818′.309 — dc23
[B]
2013024777

Printed in the United States of America
DOC 10 9 8 7 6 5 4 3 2 1

To Dave Eggers,
who gave me my first break as a writer

Contents

Edgar Allan Poe

The Child of Fortune

OR MANY DECADES, the night of January 19 would bring a single mysterious visitor to a Baltimore graveyard: dressed in black and hidden by a hat and scarf, he'd raise a birthday toast and then leave behind a bottle of cognac and three roses at the stone marking the original burial site of Edgar Allan Poe. He has never been identified, and the tradition ended in 2009 amid claims that the original "Poe Toaster" had died years earlier. Curious onlookers and reporters still stake out the graveyard each year, though, and pretenders have continued to make the homage ever since, sometimes finding that other toasters have already beaten them to the grave earlier in the evening. That seems entirely fitting. An old graveyard at midnight, mysterious visitors, false identities, and an unsolved mystery: one suspects Poe himself would approve of the whole affair.

But to understand Poe — the father of detective fiction, the master of horror, the critic, the novelist, the poet, the tragic artist — one might better turn their gaze from those shadowy figures in the graveyard and instead watch the *Baltimore Sun* reporter taking notes from the perimeter. There, and not amid the weathered tombstones, is the reality of the living and working writer. Poe's reputation was not earned through tragedy, but in spite of it: he was a careful craftsman of words, and a man whose deep dedication to understanding art is often obscured by the drama around his life.

Edgar Allan Poe was born into a world of artists struggling to survive. His father was the mercurial namesake son of one of Baltimore's great patriots of the Revolution — but instead of the law career that had been marked out for him, David Poe Jr. took to the stage. In 1806 he married Eliza Arnold, who had theater in her blood — the child of English actors, she'd first appeared onstage by the age of nine, and was orphaned at fourteen as her family toured America. Renowned for her singing voice and her dancing, Eliza was often given lead parts reserved for pretty, magnetic young actresses; her Shakespearean roles alone included Juliet, Desdemona, Ariel, and Cordelia. A surviving cameo portrait shows a delicate woman with dark ringlets and a bemused look; she was lauded by one theater patron as "a brilliant gem in the Theatrick crown."

David was not quite her equal onstage. Rarely the lead, he tackled bit parts in Boston and New York theaters with earnestness, sometimes mumbling lines when flustered. The greatest role he ever landed, perhaps, was as Eliza's husband. When they married, she was nineteen and newly widowed, and now she wasted no time in starting a family. Three children followed in quick succession in 1807, 1809, and 1810: Henry, Edgar, and Rosalie.

Life in the theater was precarious, and after Edgar's birth on January 19, 1809, David was back onstage the next night at the Boston Theatre. Eliza, after "the recovery of her recent confinement," was treading the boards again just three weeks later. Soon they were leaning upon Boston's theatergoers with shows "For the Benefit of Mrs. Poe." Theater had a culture of such shows — perusing Boston newspapers that same month, one finds benefits for Mrs. Poe, Master Payne, Messrs. Stockwell and Barnard, Mr. and Mrs. Barnes, and Miss Worsall — a testament to the changeless struggle of artists to earn their way.

In their scramble for desperately needed money, neither parent could care for Edgar much. Scarcely a month after his birth, Edgar joined his brother, Henry, with their grandparents in Baltimore. He rejoined his parents six months later, in New York City, but the infant's new home was not an entirely happy one. Manhattan newspapers tolerated neither mumblers nor stumblers: one critic labeled David Poe a "muffin face" and mercilessly dubbed him "Dan Dilly" after he mispronounced a character named "Dandoli." Over the next two years, David Poe would respond with the melancholy predictability of foolish men: he got angry, he drank, and then he abandoned his wife and children. There was no reconciliation, nor could there be: David died in obscurity soon afterwards.

He left behind the newborn and sickly Rosalie, born after a theatrical run by her mother in Virginia — and soon Mrs. Poe herself was ailing. In November 1811, one Richmond local wrote: "Mrs. Poe, who as you know is a very handsome woman, happens to be very sick, and (having quarreled and parted with her husband) is destitute." A visitor recalled finding the children "thin and pale and very fretful," and being hushed by an old nurse with nips of opium and gin-soaked bread. Soon an ominous notice appeared in the *Richmond Enquirer* for another benefit show: "Mrs. Poe, lingering on the bed of disease and surrounded by her children, asks your assistance, and *asks it for perhaps the last time.*"

This was no exaggeration. A month later, one could spot the well-to-do Richmond merchant John Allan and his wife, Frances, spending the Christmas holiday at a friend's plantation — and toddling alongside them through the snow, a bewildered and newly adopted young orphan named Edgar.

He was now, an aunt wrote, "truly the Child of fortune."

Poe was born into a life of art, but adopted into one of commerce, and from this uneasily mixed parentage, both the name and the career of Edgar Allan Poe would emerge. For just as Eliza Poe was a great talent in her profession, so was John Allan in retailing. At the Richmond dry goods warehouse of Ellis & Allan, one could find everything from sheet music to coal shovels, "Chamber door Locks" to window glass, and heaped piles of "superfine Broadcloths and Kersemeres."

A bluff and hardheaded merchant, Allan was a Scotsman turned American, adopted by the country he'd emigrated to in 1795. Though one contemporary described him as "rather rough and uncultured," Allan also possessed more subtle qualities. Like many a hard-driven merchant, he'd never had a college education, and could seem alternately dismissive and ardent in his admiration for culture. "Gods! What would I not give, if I had his talent for writing!" he once wrote of Shakespeare. The survival of 615 volumes of Ellis & Allan commercial correspondence do not hint at a man with much time to fulfill such dreams. But he acquired the trappings of culture for his prosperous household: they would never lack for Shakespeare, nor for a costly Rees's *Cyclopedia* or a piano in the parlor.

The Allans had both been orphaned as children themselves. At thirty-one, John was now a respectable Richmond merchant with no offspring—none by his rather frail wife, Frances, at least. It was Frances who pressed for taking in little Edgar, and by 1812 the Allan ledgers show the telltale touches of parenthood: amid the fine horses and casks of brandy are orders for diminutive suits of clothing, doctor's visits for croup, and a child-size bed.

Edgar was, visitors recalled, "a lovely little fellow, with dark curls and brilliant eyes, dressed like a little prince." Yet he was the prince of an uncertain peerage. John hadn't formally adopted him—perhaps imagining that Poe's relatives would decide to raise him, as they had with his siblings, Henry and Rosalie. But as weeks passed into months and months into years, Edgar Poe disappeared from records, and in his place appeared a new identity: *Edgar Allan.* When John Allan set out in August 1815 to open a London branch of his firm, he was joined by his wife and his spirited six-year-old boy. Interrupting Allan as the merchant drafted a letter to confirm his arrival, Poe's voice materialized on paper for the first time.

"Edgar says *Pa, say something for me*," Allan wrote in bemusement to his business partner. "*Say I was not afraid coming across the sea.*" Edgar took a child's delight in the thirty-four-day voyage, even as his family was distinctly the worse for wear from seasickness.

Arriving in London mere months after the end of both the War of 1812 and the surrender of Napoleon, the Allans found an empire staggered with debt and swarming with wounded veterans, yet poised upon the brink of the most powerful and peaceful decades that Britain had ever known. It was here, at the center of a new British empire, that Edgar would have many of his first childhood memories. Just before Halloween that year, a letter written by Allan gave the first real glimpse of Edgar. The family was "by a snug fire" in their parlor, he wrote, with Mrs. Allan sewing and "Edgar reading a little Story Book"—perhaps *Sinbad the Sailor* or *Jack and the Beanstalk,* both of which had recent children's editions. When he wasn't reading, Edgar could amuse himself with his mother's parrot, which the family had taught to recite the alphabet.

Such pleasant idylls could not last, though. Edgar was packed off to boarding schools; and there, a foreign child of seven, he fell asleep at night under a strange roof in a strange land, and woke to eat among yet more strangers. He was so desperate to flee the grounds and hike back to London that for a time a cousin had to shadow him just to keep him from escaping.

In his copy of *The English Spelling Book,* though, he could lose himself in the beauties of language. His textbook was designed to inculcate the morals and mores of its time, with lessons including such edifying dialogue as "We poor folk must not eat white bread, Miss." But it was also a textbook from the very height of the Romantic era, and one of the book's earliest exercises is this weirdly lovely description of a dead fly: "Alas! It is dead. It has been dead for some time. Its wings, you see, are like gauze, and its head looks like gold and pearl, but far more bright its eyes! The fly can not move its eyes; so it has more than you can count, that it may see all round it. They look like cut glass." Later the book treats readers to the tale of a brother who, frightened to insanity by his prank-loving sisters, promptly murders his father.

Edgar Allan read these books eagerly. He had a natural aptitude for language, with his father singling it out for praise in an 1818 letter back to the States: "Edgar is a fine Boy and reads Latin pretty sharply."

By late 1819, a shaky economy briefly had the Allan family down to their last hundred pounds, and they decided to return to America the following summer. At least a few people in Britain would remember Edgar long after he left. When one of his schoolmasters, Rev. John Bransby, was asked decades later about Poe, he politely recalled the "quick and clever boy" that he still called "Edgar Allan" out of habit. But when pressed, the reverend's assessment of his long-gone pupil became more succinct.

"Intelligent, wayward and willful," he said.

In the July 22, 1820, issue of the *New-York Daily Advertiser,* amid the ads for "Harps and Piano-Fortes Cheap!!" and announcements of "Stollenwerck's Mechanical & Picturesque Panorama," readers could find the passenger manifests of the latest ships in harbor. Travel from across the sea remained momentous enough to warrant a mention in the news, but that day's arrivals would bring the first appearance in print of five particularly auspicious letters: *E A Poe.* Returning to the States after five years away, the boy was no longer "Master Allan," but a strapping eleven-year-old with a new name and identity. His conscious memories of childhood belonged to London, as did his manners, education, and speech; returning to Richmond, Virginia, Poe now found himself a foreigner in his own land.

Still reeling from the Panic of 1819, for a time John Allan moved his family under the roof of his business partner, Charles Ellis. During the day, Edgar would roam the woods and fields of Richmond, often with Ellis's young son Thomas in tow. "He taught me to shoot, to swim, and to skate, to play bandy," Ellis later recalled, "and I ought to mention that he once saved me from drowning." Edgar also knew how to make trouble, and received a hiding for shooting at a neighbor's birds; when stuck back in the house, Poe donned a sheet to interrupt his father's whist game dressed as a ghost, and chased Thomas's sister with an imitation snake "until it almost ran her crazy."

At school, Poe showed a more thoughtful side. Placed in the academy of a local Latin scholar, he became captivated by the *Odes* of Horace. First published in 23 BC during the zenith of Roman power, their very existence proved one ode's promise that poetry was "A monument more durable than brass / And higher than the loftiest pyramid . . ." Poe memorized them, reciting the Latin "so often in my hearing," recalled one classmate, "that I learned by sound the words of many, before I understood their meaning."

Poe's competitive side manifested itself even in poetry — *especially* in poetry. Schoolboys amused themselves by "capping verses," or quoting a line of Latin poetry at a rival who then had to respond with another quote whose first letter matched the last previous letter. The trick was to use a letter like *X*, which was easy to end a line with, but hard to start on. A surviving duel of Horace and Juvenal quotes from the era, slightly condensed, gives a feel for it:

"*Nec vaga cornix.*"
"*Xanthia Phoceu, prius insolentum.*"
"*Mittit venenorum ferax* — trouble you for another x."

"*Xerxis et imperio bina coisse vada*."
"*Ad summum, nec Maurus erat, nec Sarmata, nec Thrax* ...
I'll trouble you once more to cap me with an x."

And so on, until someone emerged victorious at having stumped the other for an answer. It was not a talent Edgar could extend to all subjects — "he had no love for mathematics," his schoolmaster Joseph Clarke mused — but in poetry, he brooked no rival. Before Poe turned thirteen, his father had already approached Dr. Clarke with an unusual question.

"Mr. Allan came to me one day with a manuscript volume of verses," the schoolmaster recalled, "which he said Edgar had written, and which the little fellow wanted to have published." Clarke dissuaded him, arguing that "Edgar was of a very excitable temperament," and that the attention might turn the boy's head altogether. The manuscript circulated among his classmates, though, with one even borrowing pages to take home and show to his mother. Of their contents, they were recalled as "chiefly pieces addressed to the different little girls of Richmond."

Women did not exactly diminish in his attentions in the next year or two. He felt, he later explained, "the first, purely ideal love of my soul" toward Jane Stannard, the pretty and kindly mother of one of his classmates. Her mind and health were faltering, though, and Poe was thrown into turmoil by her death in April 1824. He sought solace once again in poetry; his earliest surviving scrap dates from this year, when he picked up a sheet of calculations from his father's office and scratched three lines onto it:

— Poetry. by . Edgar A. Poe —
Last night with many cares & toils oppress'd
Weary, I laid me on a couch to rest —

His foster father, apparently surprised by a fifteen-year-old's capacity to turn moody, quickly blamed Edgar's friends. "He does nothing & seems quite miserable, sulky & ill-tempered to all the Family," Allan wrote that autumn. "How we have acted to produce this is beyond my conception. . . . I fear his associates have led him to adopt a line of thinking & acting very contrary to what he possessed when in England."

Allan might not have understood his son, but he had Edgar's friends right. The boy was literally *acting* different around them. Poe had a fondness for singing that he'd inherited from his mother, and remained curious about his theatrical birth parents; brief visits by his older and long-separated brother, Henry Poe, only served to remind him of his past. With Mrs. Stannard's son and another classmate, Edgar formed a Thespian Society, putting on the occasional production like *Julius Caesar* for one-cent admission. And while his classmates could admire Poe for his athleticism — he had become a lean, swift runner and powerful swimmer — they were less sure what to make of his theatrics.

"Of Edgar Poe it was known that his parents had been players, and that he was dependent on the bounty that is bestowed upon an adopted son," his classmate John Preston recalled. "All this had the effect of making the boys decline his leadership; and on looking back on it since, I fancy it gave him a fierceness he would otherwise not have had."

But the standing of Poe and his adoptive family was about to change. Ever since his ill-fated venture in London, John Allan had barely kept his creditors at bay, and his partnership with Ellis finally dissolved in 1824. But the following year brought both shock and relief: the death of a rich uncle, and a one-third share of his estate. Almost instantly, Allan became one of the wealthiest men in Richmond; the creditors disappeared, and Allan bought a fine brick mansion.

Strolling through its tearoom and mirrored ballroom, Poe

now had the dazzling prospect of the life of a wealthy scion before him. He would become a Virginia gentleman; for rather than returning to Britain to finish his education, he no longer even needed to leave the state. The year before, Thomas Jefferson had opened one of the great projects of his life, the University of Virginia. In the school's second year of existence, *Edgar Allan Poe* was inscribed as student number 136 in its enrollment book.

For the first few months, it seemed to be going well.

"I this morning received the clothes you sent me," Edgar wrote from Charlottesville to his father, "viz an uniform coat, six yards of striped cloth for pantaloons & four pairs of socks — The coat is beautiful and fits me exactly."

Poe's concerns were the usual ones of a college student away from home, including a shortage of money so immediate that he asked for another hundred dollars within a week of arriving on campus, and discovering he needed clothes and other items that he'd left at home. ("Send me a copy of the *Historiae* of Tacitus — it is a small volume — also some more soap.") He'd also left a girlfriend back in Richmond, Elmira Royster, whom he had met over the summer. He dutifully wrote letters to her, and soon joined the long college tradition of wondering why they went unanswered.

Still, his new college digs — the auspiciously chosen Room 13 of his dorm — represented a new freedom for him, and an artistic sanctuary. Amid his spartan wooden furnishings and flickering tallow candles were copies of Voltaire and *Historie Ancienne* that he'd borrowed from the college library, and a prized illustrated copy of Lord Byron. Poe used one of the book's plates to draw a life-sized portrait on his dorm-room ceiling; it had only been two years since the great Romantic poet died while joining the Greek war for independence, and Poe had a seventeen-year-old's appreciation for a scandalous artist's glorious death.

The scandals outside his door were a different matter. On a campus where the rotunda was still half-built, and the library's books hadn't even been catalogued, Jefferson had created an extraordinarily forward-thinking experiment in education — a school with an entirely elective curriculum, and self-policed through a student honor code. The result during Poe's time there was sometimes less like Utopia than a barbaric state of nature. One UVA student horsewhipped a classmate over a card game, while another pair took to libeling each other so furiously, Poe marveled, that "every pillar in the University was white with scratched paper" from their opposing flyers.

Others sank their teeth into each other in a more literal manner.

"I saw the whole affair — it took place before my door ..." Poe wrote to his father of one savage fight that resulted in bite wounds. "I saw the arm afterwards — It was really a serious matter — It was bitten from the shoulder to the elbow — and it is likely that pieces of flesh as large as my hand will be obliged to be cut out."

Still, Poe tried to fit in by gulping down the favored campus drink of peach brandy, emptying his glasses at a single toss. But even then, Poe seemed curiously aloof — and, perhaps, just a little too serious about his art. After reading aloud to classmates a short story featuring a character named Gaffy, it instantly stuck to an exasperated Poe as his college nickname.

"My impression was and is that no one could say that he *knew* him," a classmate mused years later of "Gaffy." "He wore ... a sad, melancholy face always, and even a smile, for I don't remember his ever having laughed heartily, seemed forced." It was a trait that others noticed in Poe. "He was a beautiful boy — Not very talkative," his girlfriend Elmira observed. "When he did talk, though, he was pleasant, but his general manner was sad." Perhaps, as he sometimes hinted, his melancholy disposition came from his birth parents and their tragic end; but if so, it was deepened by John Allan's refusal to formally adopt him, which left Edgar's place in the world always slightly uncertain.

Yet Poe was at ease in the classroom. He'd signed up for two courses — Ancient Languages and Modern Languages, which met at alternating mornings on a 7:30–9:30 schedule. Poe coasted through them, relying on a natural ability so great that he went into class nearly unprepared. His freshman year came to an end in December 1826, with exams administered by no less than Jefferson's two fellow Republican successors: James Madison and James Monroe. Poe scored top marks in Latin and solid ones in French.

The end of the school year, though, was not a happy one. Poe crossed paths with William Wertenbaker, a fellow student who also served as the campus librarian — a sympathetic ear on a campus where the young poet had never entirely fit in. He found "Gaffy" so ready to abandon campus that he'd smashed up his dorm-room furniture to save on buying firewood for his final nights there.

"It was a cold night in December," Wertenbaker said, "and his fire having gone pretty nearly out by the aid of some tallow candles, and the fragments of a small table which he broke up for the purpose, he soon rekindled it, and by its comfortable blaze I spent a very pleasant hour with him."

Poe still hadn't turned eighteen, and was younger than most of his classmates, but Wertenbaker knew him as a fine scholar — he'd seen Poe take on an extra-credit assignment at translating Italian poetry, one that none of his classmates had bothered with. What the librarian hadn't known was that their young genius was in deep trouble. As Poe sat by the embers of his table, he revealed his secret: that after being sent to college without enough money, he'd resorted to the quickest and most disastrous solution. Poe was up to his eyes in gambling debt.

"He spoke with regret of the large amount of money he had

wasted and of the debts he had contracted," Wertenbaker wrote. "He estimated his indebtedness at $2,000, and though they were gaming debts, he was earnest and emphatic in the declaration, that he was bound by honor to pay at the earliest opportunity."

Biographers ever since have puzzled over why Allan failed to give Poe enough money. It is hardly a mystery to any first-generation student. John Allan was an immigrant who never attended college; what he understood was business, secondary schools, and the occasional tutor fee. In the same issue of the *Richmond Enquirer* that showed Poe's name atop a column of UVA results, there were over a dozen ads for local finishing schools — that was the world Allan knew. Of the time and money necessary for college, and its cultivation of sheer intellectual curiosity, he was ignorant; when Poe complained about being underfunded, Allan shot back that his son had wasted his education on things like reading *Don Quixote*.

Poe arrived back in Richmond for the holidays with his deadbeat reputation preceding him: the letters to his girlfriend were intercepted by her father, and creditors lurked at social gatherings, ready to take Edgar aside for a quiet word. Worse still, Charlottesville merchants dunned the Allans with Edgar's bills for clothes, laundry, and firewood. John Allan could certainly afford to pay them — in fact, he'd just been named to the board of the Bank of Virginia. But he refused, pointedly referring creditors back to his penniless teenaged son.

Poe found the only opportunity given to him was an unpaid job in his father's warehouse, where he might learn a practical trade. The boy who had been translating Latin and French to former presidents just days earlier now found himself facing virtual servitude to the Allans.

"Mr. Allan was a good man in his way, but Edgar was not fond of him," a family acquaintance later recalled. "He was sharp and exacting, and with his long, hooked nose, and small keen eyes looking from under shaggy eyebrows, he always reminded me of a hawk. I know that often when angry with Edgar he threatened to turn him adrift, and that he never allowed him to lose sight of his dependence upon his charity."

Technically, Edgar remained a guest in Allan's house, for he'd never been formally adopted — he was still, strictly speaking, an indigent orphan. When a constable showed up at the mansion in March 1827 to serve Poe for unpaid debts, he was astounded to walk away empty-handed, with the report that he could "find no property to levy execution on." The next step was quite possibly jail — and by the end of the week, Poe was on the run.

He didn't go very far at first. Kicked out by his father, he found a room in a Richmond inn and wrote a scathing declaration: "My determination is at length taken — to leave your house and endeavor to find some place in this wide world — to be treated — not as *you* have treated me." But one day later, out of food and money, a second letter by the scorned boy turned heartrending. "I am in the greatest necessity, not having tasted food since Yesterday morning. I have no where to sleep at night, but roam about the Streets — I am nearly exhausted . . ." At the end of the letter is a single ragged and unpunctuated line of postscript: *I have not one cent in the world to provide any food*

And then — just like that — Edgar Allan Poe disappeared.

"I'm thinking Edgar has gone to Sea to seek his own fortunes," John Allan noted offhandedly a week later, sounding remarkably unconcerned. Yet that spring, Peter Pease, a Virginian visiting the docks of Boston, recognized a curiously familiar countenance in a shabbily dressed warehouse clerk named Henri Le Rennet.

"Edgar!" Pease innocently hailed, and the clerk frantically pushed him into an alleyway.

"Poe begged him not to speak his name aloud," a relative re-called, "giving for his reason that 'he had left home to seek his fortune, and until he had hit it hard he preferred to remain incognito.'"

Fortune had thus far eluded him. "Henri" was cheated out of his pay by his warehouse boss; after he then landed a job as a commodities reporter at a Boston newspaper, the firm collapsed, along with his paycheck. Spurned by his foster family, Poe found some solace in recalling his scattered siblings and his old love of poetry. He'd only ever had a few meetings with his older brother, Henry Poe, whose career as a sailor and aspiring poet seemed curiously yoked to his own. That January, Henry published his first poems in the *Saturday Evening Post,* and their kid sister, Rosalie, had written some poems, too. For this achingly brief moment in 1827, the three children of David and Eliza Poe were united again in poetry.

Broke, despairing, his landlady ready to throw him out — facing homelessness and oblivion at eighteen — a sheaf of poems had become Edgar's last chance at leaving any earthly trace. With the little money he had, the self-styled Mr. Le Rennet found an aspiring local printer as young as himself and commissioned about fifty copies of the slim, anonymous volume that looked to be his first and last work: *Tamerlane and Other Poems. By A Bostonian.*

An obscure forty-page chapbook, *Tamerlane* almost begged to be overlooked, a judgment at first glance endorsed by the author himself. "The greater part of the Poems which compose this little volume were written in the year 1821–2, when the author had not completed his fourteenth year," the still-anonymous poet announced in a brief preface, by way of excusing the verses.

Biographers often assume, on no particular grounds, that Poe's anonymity and the claim of juvenilia were to distance himself from criticism of the poems — a curious belief given Poe's lifelong immodesty regarding his own talents. In fact, the evidence of Poe's own word and those of his Richmond contemporaries was that 1821–2 was indeed when he first began seeking to publish his poetry. The poems he brought to Boston may have been much revised or altogether new, but they were the fulfillment of a dream that he'd held since he was twelve. And his recourse to a pseudonym is easily explained: he was dodging creditors. It took another six years for federal law to ban the use of debtor's prisons; revealing himself on a title page would expose Poe to far greater dangers than mere bad reviews.

Most of his volume's poems dwelled on the standard subjects of a young poet still in thrall to Romantics like Lord Byron and Thomas Moore: youth, love, lost youth and lost love, and the obliterating passage of time and ambition. "I have been happy — tho' but in a dream," he proclaims in his poem "Dreams," and his closing poem "The Happiest Day" lays out the crushing sense of loss more plainly:

> *The happiest day — the happiest hour*
> *My sear'd and blighted heart hath known,*
> *The highest hope of pride, and power,*
> *I feel hath flown.*
>
> *Of power, said I? yes! such I ween*
> *But they have vanish'd long alas!*
> *The visions of my youth have been —*
> *But let them pass.*

To see in all this the dashed dreams of a would-be Virginia gentleman is a fair interpretation of the poem, and yet perhaps not a very useful interpretation of Poe himself. The life of an author may say much about a work of art; the reverse is a shakier proposition. So much depends on the subjective experience of the work — and so little of one's life may go into a particular piece —

that the use of art to fill in the blanks of biography, while tempting, is to misunderstand art and biography alike.

The loss of youth and dashed ambition were standard themes of Romantic poetry, after all; they are as unsurprising in Poe's volume as that era's thuddingly matched end-rhyme, right down to jangling pairs of "pass" with "grass," and "night" with "light." His vocabulary could also turn vague and platitudinous, with plenty of "visions," and enough talk of "a dream" and "dreams" that both turn up as poem titles.

What was less conventional in Poe's poetry was his mastery at creating dramatic pauses through em-dashes. Employing punctuation as the textual equivalent of musical rests — a comma counting for one beat, a dash for two, a colon for three, and a period for four — was an eighteenth-century tradition that Poe had learned in childhood, where this rhythmic approach to language still formed part of his earliest lessons from *The English Spelling Book.* But even more striking was his use of a first-person narrative "I" addressing "you," and not simply as an author addressing the reader. After variously living as Edgar Poe, Edgar Allan, and Edgar A. Poe, he was now living under his fourth identity as Henri Le Rennet — and he had learned how to skillfully adopt the voices of fantastic, entirely fictitious personae.

Nowhere was this clearer than in his titular poem, "Tamerlane"—a work that Poe already knew was his most accomplished and mature. In it, his narrative persona has gained a precise name and voice; his meter and rhyme have shifted to more closely mimic conversation, subtly undergirding the lines rather than jacketing them. The grand subject of the rise, fall, and exile of the legendary Turkish conqueror, too, is different — though to a reader in the present, there is perhaps nothing anonymous or mythic about the "Bostonian" here. The very first words of "Tamerlane" seem to mimic the miseries of a spurned son: "Kind solace in a dying hour ! / Such, father, is not (now) my theme —"

Tamerlane, in Poe's use of a fictive tradition, now faces his deathbed regretting a life of ruthless conquest pursued at the expense of his young love — "a kingdom for a broken heart." The disastrous loss of youth lurks throughout the poem ("I have not always been as now"), along with the relentless approach of mortality:

> *Father, I do firmly believe —*
>   *I know — for Death who comes for me*
>   *From regions of the blest afar*
> *Where there is nothing left to deceive,*
>   *Hath left his iron gate ajar . . .*

Yet, for many years, it was not just life but *Tamerlane and Other Poems* itself that seemed to disappear through that deathly iron gate. Poe's little book did not meet with a single review; like many first works of poetry, it found only crushing silence. But for a miserable clerk on the Boston docks, eking out enough money to print fifty anonymous copies, this may never have been the point. Whether the world at large recognized him or his work, something had changed inside the shifting identity of the fugitive Edgar Allan Poe — something irrevocable.

He was an author now.

2

Manuscript Found in a Bottle

B Y THE TIME *Tamerlane and Other Poems* came out, anyone seeking its author on the Boston docks would find
that Henri Le Rennet had simply ... *disappeared*. One
Virginia debt collector reported to a creditor that their deadbeat had likely run off to a foreign revolution.

"Poe has gone off entirely, it is said, to join the Greeks," he
wrote despairingly. "He had as well be there as anywhere else, I
believe, for he appears to be worthless."

Had they consulted the manifests of ships leaving Boston,
though, they may have spotted a curiously familiar name among
a group of new army recruits headed for Fort Moultrie, South
Carolina. After months of scraping by, the eighteen-year-old
Poe assumed his fifth incarnation on May 16, 1827: Private Edgar A. Perry, age twenty-one. Both his name and his false trail
were drawn straight from that week's newspapers. There *was*
a relief ship from the Greek Committee of Boston about to
leave the harbor; as for his name, though one of his old UVA
classmates has been suggested as an inspiration, a simpler explanation also lay in that week's Boston papers: excited reports
of the London departure of polar explorer Captain William
Parry, whose HMS *Hecla* was bound for the North Pole. Poe
had a longstanding fascination with the mysterious poles of the
earth; some had even theorized that they were giant holes into
which humans venturing too close would irretrievably disap-

pear. For an adventurous young man reinventing himself, what better new name to take?

The voyage to Fort Moultrie was so rough that the army lost a sister ship in the storm, and Poe's regiment arrived thankful to escape with their lives. Yet the island fortress seemed as barren a destination as Captain Parry's Arctic: "It consists of little else but sea sand," Poe later wrote, with "no trees of any magnitude" and "some miserable frame buildings, tenanted, during summer, by fugitives from Charlestown dust and fever."

Still, military life suited him curiously well; the US Army has the distinction of being the only institution to steadily support and appreciate the talents of Edgar Allan Poe while he was still alive. Assigned to an artillery battery and trained to prepare munitions, "Perry" now had food, clothing, shelter, and a reliable if modest salary of ten dollars a month. Before two years of his five-year stint were finished, he'd already risen to the highest enlisted rank of Regimental Sergeant Major.

He continued writing and revising his poems, even appearing surreptitiously in magazines. His brother, Henry Poe, having landed some poems of his own in the short-lived *North American* magazine, quietly slipped in two of Edgar's poems under his own "W.H.P." byline — a necessary disguise, as Edgar was still on the run from creditors. A brief prose piece titled "A Fragment" also ran under Henry's byline in the November 3, 1827, issue, though it was an uncharacteristically fevered first-person account by a despairing man about to shoot himself in the head: "Heavens! my hand does tremble — No! tis only the flickering of the lamp.... No more — the pistol — I have loaded it — the balls are new — quite bright — they will soon be in my heart — Incomprehensible death — what art thou? . . ." It's quite unlike anything else published by Henry Poe. It is, though, remarkably similar to the mad, insistent narrators of Edgar's later work. Hidden for centuries under Henry's name, "A Fragment"

might instead be among the eighteen-year-old Edgar Allan
Poe's first published works of fiction.

As 1828 came to a close, Poe chafed at a five-year enlistment
that offered no further advancement; his best hope lay in peti-
tioning for a paid substitute to take his place so that he could attend West Point for officer training. Breaking a long silence to
write to John Allan, Edgar contritely revealed his ruse and asked
for help — "I am altered from what you knew [of] me, & am no
longer a boy tossing about on the world without aim or con-
sistency." Though Allan ignored him at first, the death of his
wife, Frances, that February softened him; in the days after her
funeral, the adoptive father and son warily reconciled. With a
grudging letter from Allan and sterling recommendations from
his commanding officers ("His habits are good and interly [sic]
free from drinking," one added rather hopefully), Edgar A.
Perry was honorably discharged in April 1829.

Poe spent much of that year with blood relatives in Baltimore, killing time while angling for an acceptance to West
Point. The pleasure of reuniting with his brother, Henry, was
tempered by their dire situation. Edgar wrote to John Allan that
he was "without one cent of money — in a strange place. . . . My
grandmother is extremely poor and paralytic. My aunt Maria if
possible still worse & Henry entirely given up to drink & unable
to help himself, much less me —"

Amid this squalor, Poe spent his scarce pennies to mail poems to magazines, though to limited effect; the prominent editor N. P. Willis informed *American Monthly* readers that he
took pleasure in burning one unnamed submission ("It is quite
exciting to lean over eagerly as the flame eats in upon the letters") and then mortifyingly quoted lines from Poe's "Fairy-
Land." *Yankee* magazine editor John Neal, while not ready to
publish Poe, at least encouraged him; if Poe could sustain his
best lines across an entire poem, he wrote, "he will deserve to

stand high — very high — in the estimation of the shining brotherhood" of poets.

Poe was determined to try. At the end of 1829 he issued a small run of a new volume: *Al Aaraaf, Tamerlane, and Minor Poems*. This time, perhaps thanks to reluctant financial help from John Allan, he no longer needed to hide himself: "BY EDGAR A. POE," the cheap paper cover proudly proclaimed.

Inside, his handful of readers found greatly revised poems from his first volume, along with the unfinished first half of his title opus, "Al Aaraaf." A 264-line reverie that muddles astronomical discoveries by Tycho Brahe with vague invocations of the Koran, "Al Aaraaf" is the archetypal artistic sophomore slump, a pretentiously footnoted mess whose reach far exceeds its grasp. But it was the right kind of mess for an artist to have. To grow as a writer requires ambition — and "Al Aaraaf" was certainly ambitious. But above all, an author must write passionately and edit dispassionately. Poe's willingness to ruthlessly strip down and rebuild his old poems showed a dedication to craft that a professional must have, one that quickly wilts most amateurs.

His professionalism did not extend to his work at West Point. Poe enrolled in June 1830, expecting to breeze through officer training, and was shocked to find his enlisted experience of little use. Subjected to a strict routine — up at sunrise, classes until four, then drills, supper, and more classes until bedtime — he began to drink again, and seethed through his courses.

"He is thought a fellow of talent here," one fellow Virginia cadet wrote back home, "but is too mad a poet to like Mathematics."

What he did like was writing mocking verses upon his instructors, much to the delight of classmates. "He would often write some of the most vicious doggerel," his roommate recalled, adding, "I have never seen a man whose hatred was so intense."

After deliberately not showing up for roll calls and classes, Poe was expelled in January 1831 — but his obvious brilliance still commanded enough regard that the academy's superintendent allowed him to take up a collection from classmates. Though he certainly could use the money himself — leaving West Point with a balance of just twenty-four cents — what Poe promised his classmates was a new volume: *Poems,* by Edgar A. Poe. Of the class of 232, 131 cadets paid $1.25 each to raise the money for it.

They did not quite get what they'd bargained for. Dedicated "to the U.S. Corps of Cadets," *Poems* revised a number of his extravagantly Romantic verses and included about a half-dozen new shorter poems. Poe considered one of them, "The Sleeper," to be among his finest work. A first hint of his fascination with the liminal states of life and death, the poem clip-clops through a standard Romantic musing on the death of a beautiful woman, before turning to a surprisingly poignant final stanza worthy of Gray or Moore:

> *Some sepulchre, remote, alone,*
> *Against whose portal she hath thrown,*
> *In childhood, many an idle stone —*
> *Some tomb from out whose sounding door*
> *She ne'er shall force an echo more,*
> *Thrilling to think, poor child of sin!*
> *It was the dead who groaned within.*

What *Poems* did not have, alas, was the satire that Poe's classmates expected for their buck twenty-five. It arrived poorly printed on coarse paper with the widest of margins — "a miserable production mechanically," Poe's roommate wrote later, "bound in green boards and printed on inferior paper, evidently gotten up on the cheapest scale." Finding one brings a small fortune today, but a very different valuation survives in what one classmate scribbled onto his copy.

"This book," he wrote, "is a damned cheat."

Broke and ill, Poe drifted to Baltimore that spring and moved back in with his relatives. They were no better off than when he'd left them a year before, and soon turned far worse: his brother, Henry, died that summer at the age of twenty-four, amid a raging cholera outbreak. Yet there were some small consolations among these miseries. Poe grew close to his aunt, Maria Clemm; she was becoming the doggedly steadfast mother he'd never had. Her young daughter, Virginia, too, increasingly came under cousin Edgar's notice.

But they remained crushingly poor. By the end of 1831, Poe was facing debtor's jail again, and writing his father to cover an eighty-dollar debt he'd contracted to help out his late brother. Allan wrote out a check — and then dithered through nearly a month of increasingly frantic letters from Edgar before finally sending it.

"What little share I had of your affection is long since forfeited," his wayward son wrote piteously, "but, for the sake of what once was dear to you, for the sake of the love you bore me when I sat upon your knee and called you father, do not forsake this only time . . ."

Along with John Allan's check, hope arrived in January 1832 in the form of a contest by the *Philadelphia Saturday Courier*. This time Poe sent prose — not poems. Although he lost, the pieces attracted enough admiration that the *Courier* ran them anyway.

Poe's early prose often reads as tired, ostentatiously learned satire. It is not for lack of craft, though: the horror satire "Metzengerstein" begins with just as portentous an invocation as in any later work, and in the dialogue of "Bon-Bon," one can already see Poe's comic mastery of rendering spasmodic conversation: "Why, sir, to speak sincerely — I believe you are — upon my word — the d — dest — that is to say I think — I imagine — I have some faint — some very faint idea — of the remarkable honor — —." But Poe would not commit to *actual* horror, and still lacked a compelling narrator. In particular, a charismatic, manic first-person presence was needed to bring alive Poe's use of dread and terrified sensation.

The first glimmerings of that talent can be seen in "A Decided Loss," whose comically unfortunate narrator proceeds to partially asphyxiate, get autopsied alive, have his nose chewed off by cats, be hung at the gallows, and then get autopsied alive again. It spoofed the "predicament tales" of *Blackwood's Edinburgh Magazine,* wild first-person fantasies of people buried alive, caught under a ringing church bell, or accidentally boiled alive in a brewery tank. Sensational art, then as now, depends on the author caring more about the sensations they are invoking than about the characters themselves — and though Poe could mock the form, he hadn't learned how to transcend it.

It didn't help that the *Philadelphia Saturday Courier* was no *Blackwood's* in its editing or its pay; it probably paid little or no money. Nor would his foster family help support his efforts; John Allan had remarried and no longer bothered to reply to his letters. Poe, who at best appears to have found some work at a local brickyard, was living on next to nothing. One could easily imagine his reaction when a local Baltimore magazine, the *Saturday Visiter,* announced in June 1833 that it was "desirous of encouraging literature" and thus running a contest with "a premium of 50 dollars for the best Tale."

Even more easily imagined was his reaction to the contest's result: he won.

Amid the many single short-story entries sent in, Poe submitted an entire collection, and the judges singled out "Ms. Found in a Bottle." A haunting maritime tale of a shipwrecked man's voyage on a ghost ship, sailing to the very edge of the po-

lar world, it purports to be a document preserved in a desperately thrown bottle as the writer teeters on an Antarctic abyss. It
was Poe's first true effort to create a believable narrator, one that
carries the reader ever further into a weird and nightmarish world.

When *Saturday Visiter* editor John Latrobe visited their
prize winner, he quickly realized just how much the fifty-dollar
award meant. "He carried himself erect and well, as one who
had been trained to it," he recalled. "He was dressed in black . . .
not a particle of white was visible. Coat, hat, boots and gloves
had evidently seen their best days, but so far as mending and
brushing go, everything had been done apparently, to make
them presentable. On most men his clothes would have been
shabby and seedy, but there was something about this man that
prevented one from criticizing his garments.

"The impression made, however," Latrobe drily added, "was
that the award in Poe's favor was not inopportune."

It also brought Poe something more precious: the regard
of an established writer, not just as a promising talent, but as a
colleague. One of the contest judges was the prominent Southern novelist John Pendleton Kennedy, a respected lawyer who
took a brotherly interest in their unsteady winner and encouraged him to work on a fiction collection that Poe had conceived, *Tales of the Folio Club.* A subscription plan to publish it
was briefly floated in the *Saturday Visiter* in late 1833, but soon
dropped; though Kennedy urged Philadelphia publisher Henry
Carey to consider the manuscript, Carey kept vacillating over it.

Poe at least landed some editorial hackwork in the magazine, which was just as well: after an ailing John Allan died in
March 1834, his will proved not to contain a single mention of
Edgar. Of the wealthy merchant's vast estate, of his eight homes
and shares in banks and gold mines, Poe would receive — nothing.

• • •

The year that followed was among the darkest and most obscure of Edgar Allan Poe's life. Henry Carey dithered endlessly over Poe's collection before finally rejecting it; meanwhile, Poe tried and failed to land a job as a teacher. "I found him in Baltimore in a state of starvation," John Pendleton Kennedy recalled, and indeed Poe once turned down a dinner invitation from Kennedy, writing back that it was "for reasons of the most humiliating nature [in] my personal appearance." Kennedy loaned him clothes and let him borrow his horse, but he couldn't give Poe a career. The first hints of that would come, though, in this simple newspaper headline that year: "PROSPECTUS of a Literary Paper to be published in Richmond, VA., by Thomas W. White, to be entitled THE SOUTHERN LITERARY MESSENGER."

America's nascent magazine industry was expanding rapidly in the 1830s; both steam-powered presses and the rise of rail and steamboat delivery meant that print runs of thousands of copies could now readily reach subscribers around the country. Amid a rush of new titles, at first blush White's was not so different: the last decade had seen both a *Southern Literary Register* and a *Southern Literary Gazette* appear and then wink out. But White assiduously cultivated contacts with respected writers, not least of which was John Pendleton Kennedy. After Kennedy successfully encouraged Poe to submit the grisly tales "Berenice" and "Morella," he wrote to White in April 1835 to strongly hint at hiring the starving author: "He is very clever with his pen — classical and scholar-like. He wants experience and direction, but I have no doubt he can be made very useful to you. And, poor fellow! He is *very* poor."

Desperate as he was, Poe presented himself as a confident professional to White. His writing had already made an impression on the rather staid *Messenger;* in "Berenice," a grieving narrator yanks the teeth out of his prematurely buried wife, while in "Morella," a deceased wife's identity takes over that of their nameless daughter. Premature burial and fluid identities were thematic obsessions for Poe, but not reflexive or unthinking ones. Writing to his new and slightly scandalized editor, he explained to White that he'd thought very carefully about the market for such stories:

> The ludicrous heightened into the grotesque: the fearful coloured into the horrible: the witty exaggerated into the burlesque: the singular wrought out into the strange and mystical. You may say all this is bad taste. I have my doubts about it. . . . But whether the articles of which I speak are, or are not in bad taste is little to the purpose. To be appreciated you must be *read,* and these things are invariably sought after with avidity.

Poe was keenly aware of the difference between what the public claims to value versus what it actually buys — something, he noted crisply, that "will be estimated better by the circulation of the Magazine than by any comments upon its contents." And yet his philosophy was not entirely mercenary. There could be artistry in such work, after all: he pointedly noted that some of Britain's finest writers were behind the sensational tales in *Blackwood's.* What was more, when White offered to pay Poe to praise the *Messenger* in other publications, he tactfully refused. He was a writer, in short, who couldn't be bought and who couldn't be shamed.

White was impressed, and in August 1835 Poe landed his first steady literary job. Though the publisher carefully skirted around an exact job title — Edgar thought himself an editor, while Thomas was not so sure — he made the young writer his right-hand man. Poe served as his personal secretary on correspondence, wrangled articles from contributors, and pounded out column after column of reviews, commentaries, and other editorial stuffing for the *Messenger*.

Inevitably, Poe's own writing suffered. "Having no time upon my hands, from my editorial duties, I can write nothing worth reading," he admitted to one correspondent. But the professional experience he was gaining was priceless, and his own writing had not been entirely rewarding lately anyway; just before coming onboard the *Messenger*'s staff, the magazine had run his comical hoax "Hans Pfaall"—the purported account of how a Dutch bellows mender escaped his creditors by flying a fantastical new hot-air balloon all the way to the moon. It was inventive, but also too absurd to take seriously. Poe was miffed when, just two months later, a far more elaborate and focused lunar hoax was perpetrated by Richard Adams Locke of the *New York Sun*.

"I am convinced that the idea was stolen from myself," Poe snapped.

It was his first fling in a long, unfortunate love affair with plagiarism accusations; though this time, at least, Poe had the sense to quickly let it drop. Locke's immensely successful account of telescope sightings of lunar man-bats and bipedal beavers cavorting around giant sapphire pyramids briefly had the *Sun*'s circulation exceeding that of the *Times* of London; eventually, even Poe admitted that Locke's work was so ingenious that "not one person in ten" suspected a fraud.

Moving to Richmond, though, brought Poe no end of more earthly concerns. Leaving his aunt Maria and cousin Virginia behind in Baltimore made Poe moderately successful—and instantly regretful. Writing to Kennedy, he admitted that even his unprecedented salary of $520 a year was no solace: "I am suffering under a depression ... I am miserable in spite of the great improvements in my circumstances." White saw his assistant's melancholy dissolving into drinking; writing in alarm to a friend, he noted Poe "was unfortunately rather dissipated. . . . I should not be at all astonished to hear that he has been guilty of suicide." He briefly fired Poe altogether — and then, after his magazine instantly ground to a halt, hired him back.

"No man is safe who drinks before breakfast!" White admonished his wayward assistant. "No man can do so, and attend to business properly."

Poe's family history did not bode well, as both his birth father and brother had been alcoholics. Edgar drank when he was anxious or distressed, and like his father, he was prone to then turning moody and argumentative. "Mr. Poe was a fine gentleman when he was sober . . ." an office boy at the *Messenger* recalled. "But when he was drinking he was about one of the most disagreeable men I have ever met." While the rhetoric of the day cast drinking as a moral failure, Edgar rarely did; when he acknowledged it at all, it was as his "illness." But it was an illness that perhaps he could recover from — and upon Edgar's return to work, his boss found him newly sober, and his nerves calmed by an assurance from his aunt and cousin that they'd move to Richmond.

Poe now had plenty of catching up to do at the *Messenger.* Starved for material after his absence, in December 1835 and January 1836 the *Messenger* published the first installments of Poe's unfinished play *Politian,* which clumsily transposed an infamous 1820s Kentucky love triangle to sixteenth-century Rome, and rendered it all in blank verse:

> LALAGE.   *A deed is to be done —*
> *Castiglione lives!*
> POLITIAN.   *And he shall die! (exit.)*
> LALAGE.   *(after a pause.) And — he — shall — die! — alas!*
> *Castiglione die? Who spoke the words?*
> *Where am I? — what was it he said? — Politian!*
> *Thou art not gone — thou are not gone, Politian!*

I feel thou art not gone — yet dare not look,
Lest I behold thee not; thou couldst not go
With those words upon thy lips — O, speak to me!

It flopped: in fact, the *Messenger* never finished the installments, and *Politian* went unproduced on stage until 1923. Like
"Al Aaraaf," the play is widely cited as one of Poe's misfires, and
like "Al Aaraaf," that is both true and beside the point. Writing
drama forced Poe to *think in scenes* — a critical requirement in
playwriting. Droll narrative musings and endlessly digressive
scholarship quickly wither in scripts, or at least they must be
credibly placed in a character's mouth.

Poe's early work indulged in rhetorical and comical extrava-
gances that interrupted the plot and kept it from being believ-
ably sustained — a weakness his mentor saw through instantly.
"You are strong enough now to be criticized," Kennedy wrote to
Poe shortly after *Politian* ran. "Your fault is your love of the
extravagant. Pray beware of it. You find a hundred intense writers for one *natural* one." Writing *Politian,* and mercilessly editing
the work of *Messenger* contributors, were just the correctives Poe
needed. With his genius at haunting narrators and an emerging
commitment to plot structure, Poe now was growing closer to a
mastery of his art.

First, though, he had to earn a living — and get married.

Edgar Allan Poe's marriage is an awkward matter for biographers; it is either obsessed about as if it provided some great
insight into his tortured narrators, or glossed over as a bit of a
family embarrassment. The long and careful development of
Poe's voice from his earlier work belies the first notion; state law
disproves the second.

Poe's cousin Virginia Clemm was thirteen years old when
he married her in May 1836; Edgar was twenty-seven. To a modern reader, the arrangement seems shocking and illegal, not

least because Virginia's age is listed on the marriage certificate as twenty-one. Edgar had known her since she was a small child, so this was an unequivocal lie. But it may not have been an entirely necessary lie. In 1836, such marriages were legal: cousins could wed, and Virginia statutes allowed women under twenty-one to be married with their parents' approval plus two witnesses; provisions of the law show it was applied as early as age twelve. Poe's aunt Maria approved his marriage to Virginia, which merely left the matter of the two witnesses. Poe's certificate has *one* witness, so the simplest explanation may be that the second didn't show up — and they fudged Virginia's age on an over-twenty-one form, which only required one witness. It was certainly not a secret ceremony; writing to John Pendleton Kennedy a few weeks later, Poe breezily comments, "I presume you have heard of my marriage."

Still: why marry a thirteen-year-old?

Legal or not, the idea is disturbing — although Poe later hinted that years passed before any consummation, and there is no hint that Virginia was ever pregnant. There may have been financial reasons to marry early, though. A scheme with his aunt Maria to run a boarding house had almost instantly fallen apart, leaving Poe in debt, but the family still had long-term prospects. He held a quixotic notion that the state of Virginia would reimburse the small fortune he believed was owed to his late grandfather, David Poe Sr.; by marrying a cousin from his father's side and becoming the beneficiary of her mother, he would effectively net a triple share of any future legal settlement.

But, unsettling as it may be today, Poe seems to have believed that Virginia was the person he was meant to be with — and sooner rather than later. Accounts of the couple are unequivocal about their deep affection for each other. "Poe was very proud and very fond of her," one visitor later recalled, "and used to delight in the round, childlike face and plump little figure, which he contrasted with himself, so thin and half-melancholy-looking, and she in turn idolized him." Poe spent much of his salary to procure her tutors, and a harp and piano; stopping by that spring, editor Lambert Wilmer found him "engaged, on a certain Sunday, in giving Virginia lessons in Algebra."

Poe had become something of a student again himself; handling nearly all of the book reviewing that year at the *Southern Literary Messenger,* he crammed on everything from phrenology ("no longer to be laughed at") to maritime navigation manuals ("attention to numerical correctness seems to pervade the work") to floral classification ("deserves the good will of all sensible persons"). When necessary, he cribbed from Rees's *Cyclopedia* and the local library to keep up the magisterial tone of editorial expertise; there was also plenty of padding provided by long excerpts.

But incoming volumes of fiction and poetry received his much closer and not always friendly attention. Along with their sensational fiction, Poe had also imbibed the *Blackwood's* ethos of reviewing: namely, to take no prisoners. He often let British works off rather lightly, but pounced on shortcomings in American literature — particularly for the misplaced nationalism, he scoffed, of "liking a stupid book the better, because, sure enough, its stupidity is American." Among those savaged by Poe for flimsy plotting, bad grammar, and weak meter were the authors of *Paul Ulric* ("despicable in every respect"), *Ups and Downs of a Distressed Gentleman* ("a public imposition"), and *The Confessions of a Poet* ("The most remarkable feature in this production is the bad paper on which it is printed").

Poe could also lavish praise; indeed, his appreciations feature some of his most careful thinking about craft. In a generally positive review of Robert Bird's satirical identity-shifting novel *Sheppard Lee,* Poe explained that a fantastical narrator must speak "as if the author were firmly impressed with the truth, yet astonished with the immensity of the wonders he relates, and for which, professedly, he neither claims nor anticipates cre-

dence." The author must commit to his conceit, in other words
—and yet must also perform a sleight of hand, and not over-
explain or make the reader conscious of when the story has shifted
into the improbable. Poe was, in fact, airing a central tenet of
his own fiction: "The attention of the author, who does not depend upon explaining away his incredibilities, is directed to giving them to the character and the luminousness of truth, and
thus are brought about, unwittingly, some of the most vivid creations of human intellect. The reader, too, readily perceives and
falls in with the writer's humor, and suffers himself to be borne
on thereby."

But it was the hatchet jobs that readers noticed—and Poe's
most savage assault was on Theodore Fay's 1835 book *Norman
Leslie*. A mediocre novel from the editor of the *New York Mirror*, logrolled by his paper and its friends, it represented everything about New York publishing that the upstart Poe resented.
His scathing review singled out lines to correct their grammar
and assailed the mistakes as "unworthy of a schoolboy." To Poe,
the attack represented "a new era in our critical literature." Others were not so sure—he was, one New York magazine suggested, "like the Indian, who cannot realize that an enemy is
conquered till he is scalped."

Poe would have occasion, if not the willingness, to regret his
reviews. The careers of the author and the reviewer mix with
deceptive and dangerous ease. Reviews are quick but paltry
money, distracting from the work that makes a writer's reputation; they are transient in their effect on readers, but lasting in
their damage to a writer's professional relations. After a month,
the magazine and the memory of the review is gone, but for the
man whose work is labeled "the most inestimable piece of bal-
derdash with which the common sense of the good people of
America was ever so openly and or villainously insulted"—as
Poe described Fay's novel—the enmity is likely permanent.

And Poe certainly needed friends in New York. In June 1836

his manuscript for *Tales of the Folio Club* came back with another crushing rejection, this time from Harper & Brothers. Too much of his collection had already been published in magazines, they explained, and what was more, "they consisted of detached tales and pieces; and our long experience has taught us that both these are very serious objections to the success of any publication. . . . republications of magazine articles, known to be such, are the most unsalable of all literary performances."

Poe was in good company: that same year, a similar rejection of *Twice-Told Tales* devastated Nathaniel Hawthorne. But what is striking is that authors receive precisely the same rejections from publishers even today. Short fiction sells poorly and is an extravagance barely tolerated even in established writers; editors are not fooled, if they ever were, by the transparent device of pawning off a collection as a singular work by contriving to frame the stories together. And an unsuccessful first work at a major publisher, then as now, is often quietly deemed the death of a career — if not the author's, then of the editor who knowingly buys a second work from them.

Poe refused to believe this at first and tried unsuccessfully to sell his collection to another publisher. But by the end of 1836, the hard truth of the Harper's rejection was obvious: his career as an author had led him to a dead end. Worse still, so had his career as an editor. Exasperated by Poe's drinking and his constant indebtedness, the publisher of the *Southern Literary Messenger* finally fired his brilliant, troublesome employee — and this time would not take him back.

Three months later, Poe stood up before a packed Manhattan hall of authors, editors, and booksellers and announced a toast. "To the monthlies of Gotham!" he called out. "Their distinguished editors, and their vigorous collaborators!"

It was one of innumerable toasts at the city's first Bookseller's Dinner; gathered together in Manhattan's stately City Hotel on March 30, 1837, authors from Washington Irving to James Fenimore Cooper were in attendance, and even an elderly Noah Webster raised a glass in the hope that "may good books *find or make* good readers." For Poe, the occasion was a dazzling introduction to his peers; having left his Richmond career in tatters, he moved his household to Manhattan to seek his fortune, and immediately found himself at the epicenter of American publishing.

He was not part of that center yet. Poe had made his name as a Southern critic, insulting some of the very authors he dined with that evening, and he remained so unknown that he did not appear in exhaustive newspaper articles about the dinner — indeed, he was only there as a guest of his new housemate, the antiquarian bookseller William Gowans. Yet Poe had good reason to be there that night, for among the publishers present was James Harper. Edgar had taken the advice of Harper's rejection letter and was now writing a novel for them.

When the first two chapters of *The Narrative of Arthur Gordon Pym of Nantucket* ran that year in *Southern Literary Messenger,* they scarcely read like a novel; the first chapter was essentially a lad's adventure of a hairbreadth's escape, the second a *Blackwood's*-style predicament story about a stowaway trapped in a pitch-black cargo hold. But now Poe became serious about writing a novel, inspiring possibly the most disciplined stretch of his life since his time in the army. Holed up in a Greenwich Village boarding house with Maria, Virginia, and Gowans, Poe stopped drinking and wrote *Pym* at a breakneck pace. "I must say I never saw him the least affected with liquor," Gowans recalled of these months. He found that Poe kept "good hours" working away at his book, tended to by his protective wife and aunt. At the end of June, Harper's filed for copyright; only an economic crash kept it waiting until 1838 to arrive in stores.

What readers found was an account that purported to be collected by Poe, but as the "true" narrative of Pym, the survivor of an extraordinary stowaway voyage to the South Pole. Or, as the subtitle exhaustively explained: *Comprising the Details of a Mutiny and Atrocious Butchery on Board the American Brig Grampus, on Her Way to the South Seas, in the Month of June 1827. With an Account of the Recapture of the Vessel by the Survivors; Their Shipwreck and Subsequent Horrible Sufferings from Famine; Their Deliverance by the Means of the British Schooner Jane Guy; the Brief Cruise of This Latter Vessel in the Antarctic Ocean; Her Capture, and the Massacre of her Crew Among a Group of Islands in the Eighty-Fourth Parallel of Southern Latitude; Together with the Incredible Adventures and Discoveries Still Further South to Which That Distressing Calamity Gave Rise.*

Pym begins matter-of-factly and gradually descends into a nightmare of piracy, murder, cannibalism, ghost ships, and a fantastical voyage to the South Pole that terminates in a mass slaughter of natives and sailors alike. Unable to extricate his protagonist, Poe simply cuts the book short as they approach the Pole, with a haunting figure confronting Pym and his companion Peters as they see what may be a giant Antarctic hole into a hollow globe: "And now we rushed into the embraces of the cataract, where a chasm threw itself open to receive us. But there arose in our pathway a shrouded human figure, very far larger in proportions than any dweller among men. And the hue of the skin of the figure was of the perfect whiteness of the snow."

It is a haunting ending; it is also a fudge, and the author knew it.

Novel writing was difficult for Poe. Although he'd blithely claimed in the *Southern Literary Messenger* that "We cannot bring ourselves to believe that less actual ability is required in the composition of a really good 'brief article,' than in a fashionable novel of the usual dimensions," he was not speaking from experience, and had little idea of how to construct extended narrative. And while it's a less obvious paste-up job than the *Fo-*

lio Club would have been, *Pym* is still essentially three novel-las stuck together: a stowaway adventure, an endurance narra-tive, and a lost-world tale. Racing to finish his book, Poe stuffed the first two sections with plagiarisms that read like schoolboy reports on everything from cargo stowage technique to pen-guin rookeries. Once Poe begins the innovative proto–science fiction of the latter third of the book, the plagiarisms vanish as well — save for the cheeky reuse of hieroglyphics, which here be-come Antarctic runes. Writing about a land where the trees and "the very rocks are novel," and where even the water is a viscous purple fluid veined "like the hues of a changeable silk," Poe's sto-rytelling becomes wildly creative.

It was this part of *The Narrative of Arthur Gordon Pym* to which the reading public truly responded; one reviewer found it "a very clever extravaganza" while another announced that "Pym's adventures have been infinitely more interesting than any before recorded." Even if some dismissed it as a humbug — which it was, and a few readers were actually fooled — the pub-lic fascination with the recent expeditions to the Antarctic, and the wild hollow-earth theories then fashionable, meant that Poe's novel attracted enough notice to be republished in Brit-ain, if not enough to warrant a second printing back home.

Poe himself was neither satisfied nor enriched. Editor Evert Duyckinck recalled that he "did not appear in his conversation to pride himself much upon it." Yet Poe was too quick to write off an admittedly flawed work, for *Pym* contains some of his most extraordinary writing. Take for instance, the apparent ar-rival in chapter 10 of a Dutch brig to "save" the castaway Pym — its sailors leaning over the railings to nod encouragingly as they approach — which proves to be an entire ship of corpses struck dead by an unknown disaster, their erect corpses only animated by the writhing and tearing of seagulls in their innards. It is a scene of horror that rivals the best of Poe's short fiction.

And yet *Pym* could not sustain him; before the book came

out, the author had moved his family yet again, this time to Philadelphia, where he desperately sought a civil service clerkship — "Intemperance, with me, has never amounted to a habit," he pleaded in one letter, adding that he had "abandoned the vice altogether, and without a struggle." When that didn't work, he haplessly trained in lithographer's work. One friend, visiting Poe's home, found the author "literally suffering for want of food."

To the extent that Poe was earning a living at all, it seems to have been from newspaper hackwork that denied him even the dignity of a byline; to this day, we scarcely know what he wrote during these months. It was disheartening and humiliating. It was also the beginning of one of the most extraordinary periods of literary genius that America has seen before or since.

3

The Glorious Prospect

B Y 1838, POE HAD BEEN writing for publication for at least eleven years — or about as long as a traditional guild artisan takes to ascend from apprentice to journeyman to master. With his latest story, Poe himself sensed the maturation of his ability. "'Ligeia,'" he would tell editor Evert Duyckinck a decade later, "is undoubtedly the best story I have written." While he wrote many other contenders for that honor, "Ligeia" was indeed the end of his journeyman days — his first unequivocal masterpiece. Its appearance in the September 1838 issue of the *American Museum,* more than any other work, marked the arrival of Edgar Allan Poe as a great American writer.

"I cannot, for my soul, remember how, when, or even precisely where, I first became acquainted with the lady Ligeia," begins his tale, and the line is a telling one. In recounting a ghostly, strong-willed first wife who entirely overtakes the body of a dying, passive second wife, "Ligeia" makes a masterly use of Poe's invocation of the vague and inexpressible to haunt the reader. "Long years have elapsed" since the events, but we do not know how many; they met in "some large, old, decaying city near the Rhine," but he does not recall which; incredibly, the narrator — himself unnamed — admits that he never knew Lady Ligeia's last name. What *is* sharply rendered is a wild phantasmagoria of settings — rooms with writhing, animate curtains; arabesque carpets; Egyptian sarcophagi; grotesque wood carvings — and an obsessive detail over the faintest and possibly hallucinatory noises and hints of color in the dying woman's cheeks.

"Ligeia" returns to two of Poe's signature themes — liminal states of life and death, and the fluidity of identity — and continues a brilliant use of gothic settings that were curiously old-fashioned even by 1838. Yet Poe does not jest with or even acknowledge these as fictional conventions; he waited until a couple of months later, in his satirical "How to Write a *Blackwood's* Article," to indulge in that. Instead, "Ligeia" was Poe's first story to absolutely sustain the voice of the narrator and a belief in the conceit. He never breaks character — not to slip in an ostentatious scholarly joke, not for a sly nudge to the reader, not for grotesque description for its own sake. This disciplined internal logic would become a hallmark of Poe's craft, and the defining characteristic of the stories that we still read today.

Not everything he wrote that autumn would pass on to such fame. That season also saw him toiling over the least-known and most confoundingly odd book in the Poe canon: *The Conchologist's First Book.*

Despite his breakthrough effort in "Ligeia," Poe lacked steady work, and his *Pym* money was long spent. However, his friend Thomas Wyatt needed a nominal author for a cheap schoolroom edition of his own *Manual of Conchology,* which his publisher Harper & Brothers had insisted on only selling in an expensive version. For fifty dollars, Wyatt bought Poe's name on the cover — and apparently some editing work inside — to retool the *Manual* into a "new" book, neatly circumventing Harper. Much as Poe needed the money, it was an unwise scheme — not least because Harper was also Poe's publisher. Any chance of his working with them again had now been squandered.

For the moment, though, the commission seemed a stroke of luck, as did a letter that arrived just weeks after the April 1839 release of Poe's would-be seashell textbook. William Burton, a comic actor with literary aspirations, had recently bought out the upstart local *Gentleman's Magazine* and rechristened it *Burton's Gentleman's Magazine* — and now, as Poe had hoped, he needed editorial help.

"Shall we say ten dollars per week for the remaining portion of the year?" Burton proposed. "Two hours a day, except occasionally, will, I believe, be sufficient for all required, except in the production of any article of your own."

A comedian might believe a monthly magazine can be edited in two hours a day, but Poe was experienced enough to know better. He took the job anyway. He needed the salary, and the bold letters that now ran across the magazine — "EDITED BY WILLIAM E. BURTON AND EDGAR A. POE" — finally gave Poe the credit he so keenly desired. It also gave him a platform for his own work — too much of one, perhaps, as Burton quickly had Poe covering everything from proofreading and fillers to book reviews. It is typical that the same September 1839 issue that ran Poe's enervating, sickly masterpiece "The Fall of the House of Usher" also ran an anonymous Poe piece on "Field Sports and Manly Pastimes," that he bylined "By an Experienced Practitioner."

The boast may not be entirely fanciful; Poe implies he was familiar with nearby Barrett's Gymnasium, which is in character with his youthful achievements in running and swimming. Sam Barrett was a boxer fond of the company of actors; there are accounts of Poe spending time in an actor's drinking salon in Philadelphia, and certainly his own boss was a prominent thespian. Why not an after-work session with them on Barrett's punching bags?

Although Poe chafed against the low manners and cheapness of his employer ("Do not think of subscribing," he snapped to a friend inquiring about Burton's magazine), the association was helping him more than he cared to admit. The same month that "Usher" appeared, his allegorical masterpiece "William Wilson" ran in a local publisher's gift annual — prosaically titled *The Gift*—in which Poe and Burton were the largest contributors. Heavily illustrated annuals were the sort of sentimental publisher's ballast that Poe disdained, but their popularity among Victorians meant he was now reaching an ever-wider audience.

He was also reaching them at the height of his powers. "The Fall of the House of Usher" is closely allied to "Ligeia" in its execution. There is the indistinct date and gothic setting; the wild and oversensitive intelligence of Roderick Usher; the terrifying confusion between living and dead; and the unsettling conviction that the very walls are alive. In "Usher," though, we are also given a sympathetic narrator—the ordinary witness to extraordinary madness, a tradition that would continue through American literature from *Moby-Dick* to *The Great Gatsby* and *On the Road*.

The story bore an unexpected ethical resemblance to another recent work, though: *The Conchologist's First Book*. Poe was becoming dangerously fond of borrowing from other authors. For the climax of "Usher"—a recitation from a fanciful old book that is uncannily matched by ghastly sounds outside Usher's chamber—Poe quietly lifted the plot of the 1828 *Blackwood's* story "The Robber's Tower." It is an irony befitting that piratical era that, perhaps unknown to Poe, both *The Manual of Conchology* and "The Robber's Tower" *also* lifted, without attribution, from earlier works.

With the publication of "Usher" and "William Wilson"—a doppelganger story worthy of Nathaniel Hawthorne, in which a dissolute protagonist slays his own conscience in the form of a namesake tormentor—Poe was emboldened to revisit the notion of publishing a collection. It helped that Washington Irving wrote to him that "I am much pleased with a tale called 'The House of Usher,' and should think that a collection of tales, equally well written, could not fail of being favorably received." But when Poe approached Philadelphia publisher Lea

& Blanchard, he met nearly the same response as before: short story collections don't make money. The publisher would risk a run of only 1,750 copies — which they soon slashed to 750 — and Poe's entire payment would be twenty author copies.

Small though its run was, it would still take Lea & Blanchard three years to unload their copies of *Tales of the Grotesque and Arabesque*.

As strident and absolute as Poe could be in critiquing poetry, his notions of fiction were far more flexible; his preface to *Tales of the Grotesque and Arabesque* gives little hint to what either term means, though one might hazard to define them as being palpable satire or absurdity, versus more subtle and earnest depictions of psychological terror. The clearest stance by Poe in his preface was, in fact, to remind readers of his disdain for nationalism. With one famous line, he brushed off reviewers applying the fashionable term of "Germanism" to his gothic work: "I maintain that terror is not of Germany, but of the soul."

His book, though, could not keep Poe afloat; indeed, since he paid to mail some of his author copies to friends, it actually cost him money. Even as *Tales* arrived in bookstores at the end of 1839, Poe took up anonymous hackwork in the least grotesque or arabesque venue possible: *Alexander's Weekly Messenger,* "the largest and cheapest family newspaper in the world." Its sister publications included the decidedly un-Germanic *Silk Grower and Farmer's Manual* and *Alexander's Premium Holy Bible.* In its pages, Poe regaled readers with the talents of his house cat — "one of the most remarkable black cats in the world — and this is saying much; for it will be remembered that black cats are all of them witches." Her witchiness, it seems, primarily manifested itself in opening the latch on Poe's kitchen door.

Poe also unleashed a different sort of terror on *Alexander's* readers: bad puns.

Why does a lady in tight corsets never need comfort?
Because she's so laced — *solaced.*

More to his taste, though, was the recent fondness in periodicals for puzzles and ciphers. Poe challenged *Alexander's* readers to stump him with substitution ciphers, which were secret
messages encoded into alternate letters, numbers, or symbols.
"We pledge ourselves to read it forthwith however unusual or
arbitrary may be the characters employed," Poe boasted, and his
dare brought in a flood of responses. Over the next six months,
he unlocked nearly one hundred cryptograms, goading readers
by declaring that "Human ingenuity cannot concoct a cipher
that human ingenuity cannot resolve."

His first reader entry would prove typical ("It gave us *no
trouble whatever,*" he scoffed), and as a secret message that was
itself a riddle, its final answer provided a dry irony that Poe
could appreciate in anonymity:

850;?9

O 9? 9 2ad; as 385 n8338d– ?† sod–3 –86a5: –8x8537 95:
370d: o– h–8shn 3a sqd?8d– ?† –og37 –8x8539 95: sod–3 o–
9 ?o–1708xah– 950?9n ?† 50537 –8x8537 95: sod–3 o– 378
n9338d– 858?† ?† 38537 –8x8537 95: sod–3 –h!!ads3– nos8 ?†
sahd37 sos37 –8x8537 95: –og37 o– 9 sdho3 ?† sahd37 sos37
95: 80;737 o– 9 !a28dshn o?!n8?853 ?† 27an8 o5:otg38– 9
2038 ?95

Poe's decoded version reads:

ENIGMA.

I am a word of ten letters. My first, second, seventh, and third
is useful to farmers; my sixth, seventh, and first is a mischie-
vous animal; my ninth, seventh, and first is the latter's enemy;

my tenth, seventh, and first supports life; my fourth, fifth, seventh and sixth is a fruit; my fourth, fifth, and eighth is a powerful implement; my whole indicates a wise man.

The answer is "Temperance."

Poe had long shown a talent for logic games, including in an earlier essay for the *Southern Literary Messenger*, "Maezel's Chess Player," which methodically debunked a bogus chess-playing automaton. But soon the flood of puzzles grew too much even for Poe—"Do people really think that we have nothing in the world to do but read hieroglyphics?" he wrote mockingly in one column.

He was indeed too busy for them: beginning in January 1840, *Burton's Gentleman's Magazine* had begun running installments of a new novel by Poe, *The Journal of Julius Rodman*. An uninspired sort of "Pym Goes West," *Rodman* deservedly ranks with *Politian* as Poe's least-known major work. He never publicly took credit for Rodman's journal, though *Knickerbocker* magazine immediately saw through the ruse: "We think we discover the clever hand of the resident editor of the *Gentleman's Magazine*, MR. E. A. POE."

They would not have long to savor the work; after Poe heard Burton was planning to sell *Gentleman's Magazine*, he began circulating a prospectus for his own magazine. *Penn Magazine* promised to be a monthly to be free of "any tincture of the buffoonery, scurrility, or profanity" of European titles — Poe made a point of apologizing for his past excesses as a reviewer — and whose "form will nearly resemble that of *The Knickerbocker;* the paper will be the equal of the *North American Review*." These were the most accomplished magazines of New York and Boston, and to create their equal in Philadelphia would be a direct challenge to *Gentleman's Magazine*. When Burton heard of Poe's plan to start a rival publication, he fired him on the spot.

After sharing the same office for over a year, the two men

could scarcely contain their anger with each other. Burton called Poe a drunk, Poe called Burton a crook, and both charges had enough truth in them to draw blood.

"Your attempts to bully me excite in my mind scarcely any sentiment other than mirth . . . ," Poe jeered at Burton. "If by accident you have taken it into your head that I can be insulted with impunity I can only assume you are an ass."

Still, Poe's impatience in proposing *Penn Magazine* had gotten the better of him. *Burton's* didn't find a buyer until October, so Poe could have squeezed out six more months of desperately needed editorial work before getting laid off. Instead, he spent much of 1840 with *Penn*'s launch endlessly deferred by insufficient funds and then by illness. *Julius Rodman* was stopped dead in its tracks by his firing and left forever abandoned. Nor did any other notable writing come from Poe that year, save for "The Man of the Crowd," an allegorical voyeur's tale haunted by urban loneliness and modern anonymity. As 1841 began, though, Poe's luck seemed to change; he claimed he was one week from delivering the first issue to the printer.

"You wish to know my prospects with the *Penn*," he wrote to one contributor. "They are *glorious*."

They did not remain so. On February 4, a run on banks sent business credit crashing; any prospect of *Penn* coming out soon was instantly annihilated. Scarcely two weeks later, George Graham, the buyer from Burton of the redubbed *Graham's Magazine,* broke the bittersweet news to his readers: *Penn* was over, but Poe was to come back as an editor at *Graham's*. What readers did not know was that Poe also brought with him a remarkable story—"something in a new key," as he put it, which he had perhaps planned to use to launch *Penn*. They were about to become the witnesses to literary history.

"It is not improbable that a few farther steps in phrenological science will lead to a belief in the existence, if not the actual discovery and location, of an organ of *analysis,*" Poe's article in the April 1841 *Graham's* began, noting that a man notably endowed in his analytical organ "is fond of enigmas, of conundrums, of hieroglyphics — exhibiting in his solutions of each and all a degree of acumen which appears to the ordinary apprehension praeternatural."

Graham's readers might have fairly assumed Poe was talking about himself; he was indeed about to revive his cryptography challenge to them, boasting in one letter that "Nothing intelligible can be written which, with time, I cannot decipher." Yet the opening lines in Poe's "The Murders in the Rue Morgue" are not about himself, but his greatest literary creation: C. Auguste Dupin, amateur detective.

So far as any literary genre can be said to have been invented by one author, Edgar Allan Poe is that author, and the detective story is that genre. True, ancestors may be claimed in everything from Voltaire to thirteenth-century Chinese literature, but in Poe's story of the mysterious and horrific double murder of a Parisian pensioner and her daughter, the conventions of the modern detective were so immediately and perfectly realized as to almost defy belief. The haughtily brilliant and eccentric protagonist; the introductory vignette to show off his deductive powers to an earnest and easily amazed sidekick; the diligent but unimaginative police baffled by seemingly conflicting clues; the impossible "locked room" crime scene; the dramatic drawing-room confrontation of a suspect — it is all there, as fully formed as the grown Athena sprung forth from Zeus.

The story had some earthly parentage, of course. Along with Poe's beloved puzzle-solving, the previous decade had also seen the rise of true-crime reporting, both in James Curtis's groundbreaking book *The Murder of Maria Marten* (1827) and James Gordon Bennett's *New York Herald* coverage in 1836 of the murder of Helen Jewett. But the story's most direct influence was the world's first actual private detective — Eugene Francois

Vidocq, a French ex-con who parlayed his criminal expertise into a still rather larcenous career on the other side of the law. Poe was mindful enough of Vidocq's fanciful *Memoirs* (1828) that he drew Dupin's name from them — and then drolly had his own Parisian detective faintly praise Vidocq as "a good guesser."

In initiating the world's most popular genre of fiction, "The Murders in the Rue Morgue" is literally the most influential short story of the nineteenth century. Poe himself knew he had written something special, though even he could hardly imagine to what degree. As he idly drew up plans for yet another story collection, this one to be called *Phantasy-Pieces,* he placed "Rue Morgue" as the lead story; yet that plan never went any further than his own desk. While the story received some warm praise upon its publication, its true importance would only slowly become apparent in the decades to follow.

Instead, Poe was kept busy with his new editorial duties; though these were lighter under Graham than with Burton, he was again swamped with reviewing, puzzling over reader cryptograms, and gathering author signatures for a magazine spread on literary autographs. He soon had the opportunity to get one in person; when Charles Dickens came through Philadelphia in 1842, Poe leapt at the chance to meet him, sending copies of his books as a calling card to Dickens's room two blocks away at the United States Hotel.

The two met twice, with Dickens not only generously promising to try to find Poe a British publisher, but also offering up a curious anecdote when talk turned to the 1794 novel *Caleb Williams:* "Do you know that Godwin wrote it *backwards* — the last volume first," Dickens mused to Poe, noting that the author then "waited for months, casting about for a means of accounting for what he had done?"

This backward construction was an authorial slight of hand that Poe understood well. Pondering what he called "tales of ratiocination"— his own name for detective stories — Poe later remarked, "People think them more ingenious than they are — on account of their method and air of method. In the 'Murders in the Rue Morgue,' for instance, where is the ingenuity of unravelling a web which you yourself (the author) have woven? The reader is made to confound the ingenuity of the suppositious Dupin with that of the writer of the story."

Yet even Poe found himself unexpectedly stumped in writing his newly created genre. In the spring of 1842, he undertook writing a sequel to "Rue Morgue" — his first sequel ever, and his first use of a recurring character. As with *Politian,* his raw material was an actual crime — in this case, the mysterious death a year earlier of Mary Rogers, popularly dubbed the "beautiful cigar girl," who clerked at a Manhattan shop frequented by writers and perhaps by Poe himself. Her disappearance, and the discovery of her body three days later in the Hudson River, occasioned paroxysms in the press about everything from gang violence to police ineptitude in failing to solve the crime. For "The Mystery of Marie Roget," Poe transposed the case to Dupin's Paris — and then, in a bizarre turn, acknowledged Mary Rogers in his story as a *separate* murder of "scarcely intelligible coincidences . . . recognized by all readers in the late murder of MARY CECILIA ROGERS, at New York."

As in his earliest works, here Poe lacks the conviction of his own fictional conceit, and falls back upon a distracting absurdity. It is a narrative substitution cipher that Poe himself would have spurned had any reader sent it in. But there are other problems with the story. For one, it is not really a story at all — it is essentially a lecture by Dupin, occupied with puncturing one newspaper after another's coverage of the case — a learned diatribe that comes disconcertingly close in tone to Poe's hatchet work as a reviewer.

If the success of "Rue Morgue" explains much about detective fiction, so does the failure of "Marie Roget." Despite the grisly double-murder it has as its subject, "Rue Morgue" possesses unexpected wit and warmth; its characters interact, examine the scene of the crime, and stage a narratively gratifying confrontation of the suspect's accomplice. "Marie Roget" has none of these. Even Dupin's unnamed sidekick is given nothing to do, save for two lines in the middle of the piece: "'And what,' I here demanded, 'do you think of the opinions of *Le Commerciel*?'"—and then, a couple of pages later—"'And what are we to think,' I asked, 'of the article in *Le Soleil*?'" Without the sidekick to act as a proxy for the reader's own queries and puzzle-solving, the story lacks any place for the reader to engage with it.

"The Mystery of Marie Roget" still possesses a special place in the history of literature: just as "Rue Morgue" marked the creation of the first modern detective in fiction, so this begins the first detective series. But the Dr. Watsons of the world might take comfort in knowing that even Edgar Allan Poe found that without a sidekick, there is only a detective—but no detective story.

Among all the vagaries of Poe's career, he had always had the safety of his modest home, and Virginia and his aunt Maria to depend on. As his wife sang at their parlor piano in early 1842, though, she suddenly began coughing up bright red splotches. The highly oxygenated blood from Virginia's lungs was an unmistakable, terrible sign—the dramatic, frightening onset of tuberculosis.

"My dear little wife has been dangerously ill," Poe wrote to a friend. "About a fortnight since, in singing, she ruptured a blood-vessel, and it was only yesterday that the physicians gave me any hope of her recovery. You might imagine the agony I have suffered, for you know how devotedly I love her."

In April 1842 Poe turned in an unsettling personal allegory of a castle's devastation by a bloody plague—"The Masque of the Red Death"—and then quit his job at *Graham's*. He put a brave face on it at first, chasing the shimmering mirage of *Penn* once again, and scoffing of *Graham's* that "my reason for resigning was disgust with the namby-pamby character of the Magazine ... the contemptible pictures, fashion-plates, music and love-tales." To an old hometown friend, though, he quietly gave a different story: his ability to concentrate, he explained, was shattered by "the renewed and hopeless illness of my wife." By midsummer of 1842, scarcely ten weeks after quitting *Graham's*, Poe contemplated bankruptcy—for the country's first modern law had gone into effect just a few months earlier, and creditors were already frantically lobbying to overturn it. Instead of leaping through this brief window of debt amnesty, Poe began to drink again; by one account, he disappeared altogether for several days and was found in the wilds outside Jersey City, "wandering around like a crazy man." His drinking was not a new problem, but it was now greatly deepened by Virginia's illness.

"Her life was despaired of," he explained later. "I took leave of her forever & underwent all the agonies of her death. She recovered partially and again I hoped. Then again — again — again & even once again at varying intervals. . . . I became insane, with long intervals of horrible sanity. During these fits of consciousness I drank, God only knows how often or how much."

Brought back home, he sobered up only to find himself more broke than ever. "I am *desperately* pushed for money," he wrote to a publisher.

From this desperation came a great potboiler—a *Blackwood's* story to top all *Blackwood's* stories. Poe could mock sensational "predicament" stories—"Should you ever be drowned or hung, be sure and make a note of your sensations—they will be worth to you ten guineas a sheet," he once wrote—but he knew they sold readily, and he had a magnificent one in "The Pit and the Pendulum." A bravura technical performance, it plays out in a dark dungeon of the Spanish Inquisition, where tortures multiply absurdly (starvation, thirst, rats, fire, moving walls, dismemberment) as the narrator largely senses the danger about him — the hissing of a pendulum blade over his body, "the odor of the sharp steel" as it approaches his face, the taste of spiced food given to him without water, the sensation of heat through his fingers as fires behind the metal walls of his prison are stoked.

It was well that he sold the story: his other great piece of fiction that season, "The Tell-Tale Heart," led a cursed existence. It is the most ideal work of Poe's art. It lacks any time or place, or indeed any thing save for a bed, a pillow, a lantern, floorboards, and a victim — the barest elements of murder. The victim gets scarcely two words in ("Who's there?") and the arresting officers none, for we are trapped in the first-person present-tense narration of an insane, monumentally self-regarding man who claims he is absolutely *sane* . . . even as the guilt of his crime begins to blot out his senses.

It is an unnerving mimicry of madness that resonates in any time or place — any, at least, save Boston in 1842. "The Tell-Tale Heart" was coldly rejected by the editor of *Boston Miscellany,* who sniffed that he might buy something "if Mr. Poe would condescend to furnish more quiet articles." This was the bitter fruit of Poe's reviewing: a year earlier he had publicly dismissed the same editor's work as "insufferably tedious and dull." Instead, he sold the piece for the launch of a new magazine, *Pioneer.* "The Tell-Tale Heart" took pride of place in the magazine's first issue, but went unpaid, as *Pioneer* collapsed almost immediately after its publisher, James Russell Lowell, fell ill.

Poe, uncharacteristically, did not insist on getting paid. "As for the few dollars you owe me . . . I may be poor, but must be very much poorer, indeed, when I even think of demanding them," he assured Lowell. For in Lowell he could see his own plight: a frightening portent, as Poe struggled to start *Penn* amid his own wife's illness. He renamed his effort *The Stylus* and wrote another prospectus, but what Poe needed now was not another magazine, but the kind of steady life that writing could not give him.

What he needed, in short, was a desk job. His mind turned to a friend's letter from the year before.

"How would you like," fellow writer Frederick W. Thomas had corresponded from Washington, D.C., "to be an office-holder here at $1,500 per year payable monthly by Uncle Sam who, however slack he may be to his general creditors, pays his officials with due punctuality. How would you like it? You stroll to your office a little after nine in the morning leisurely, and you stroll from it a little after two in the afternoon homeward to dinner, and return no more that day."

Poe liked it very much indeed: a patronage job as a clerk would pay twice what he earned at *Graham's* and sounded like an artist's idyll. Thomas was a friend of President Tyler's son and might be able to swing Edgar a Customs House job. And so it was on March 8, 1843, that Edgar Allan Poe left Philadelphia with all the nervous hope of an interviewee seeking a new job.

But when Poe got nervous, he drank.

The trouble began soon after he arrived at his hotel. Thomas was sick. Even worse, some twelve hundred applications had poured in for jobs at the Customs House. Left largely to his own devices in a strange city, Poe began to unravel.

"On the first evening he seemed somewhat excited, having been persuaded to take some Port-wine," wrote one friend. Although Poe stayed sober the next day, he soon began drinking again, woozily wearing his cloak inside-out and insulting Thomas and other potential allies — including, in one case, committing the grave error of making fun of an editor's moustache. An acquaintance, chancing upon him in the street in Washington, recalled that he was "seedy in appearance and woe-begone. . . . He said he had not had a mouthful to eat since the day previous, and begged me to lend him fifty cents to obtain a meal."

Another friend of Poe's, Jesse Dow, had now seen quite enough.

"I think it advisable for you to come and safely see him back to his home," Dow wrote to a publisher in Philadelphia. "Mrs. Poe is in a bad state of health, and I charge you, as you have a soul to be saved, not to say a word to her about him until he arrives with you."

Returning home to Philadelphia sick with regret, Poe wrote embarrassed letters of apology—"Don't say a word about the cloak turned inside out, or other peccadilloes of that nature . . . Forgive my petulance and don't believe I think all I said." If he got a clerkship, Poe promised, he would join a temperance society, and joked that "it would be a feather in Mr. Tyler's cap to save from the perils of mint julap—& 'Port wines'—a young man of whom all the world thinks so well & who thinks so remarkably well of himself."

Instead, he kept drinking. His partner for *The Stylus* withdrew his support, and Poe moved his family into more cramped quarters downtown, where a kindly landlord let the rent slide. His aunt Maria made valiant efforts to keep the house tidy and cheerfully planted beds of flowers outside, but Poe continued to toil in obscurity.

"To his neighbors his name meant very little," one local recalled years later, after he'd become famous. "Then, we felt sorry that we had not taken notice of him." But there had been little to take notice of back then, she admitted; Poe was simply a careworn-looking man, always with a grave expression on his face: "He, his wife, and Mrs. Clemm kept to themselves. They had the reputation of being very reserved—we thought because of their poverty and his great want of success."

Poe was at his lowest ebb since a decade earlier when he was disinherited from John Allan's estate. And now, as then, his salvation would come when he opened a local newspaper to discover a contest announcement.

VERY LIBERAL OFFERS, it read, AND NO HUMBUG.

The *Dollar Newspaper,* at first glance, was not a publication to impress someone who found *Graham's* to be "too namby-pamby." Just launched in Philadelphia as a "weekly family journal," it combined a carnival barker's come-on — it was for "the Farmer, the Mechanic, the Merchant, the Laborer, and Professional Man. . . . the man of business and the man of leisure, the matron and the maid. . . . the STATESMAN, the man of SCIENCE, and the POLITICIAN" — with the rather less lofty promise of "remarkable cheapness." Yet the publication was indeed thriving, and Poe was wise to submit a story to their competition, for the June 14, 1843, issue proudly announced that they had "awarded the first prize of ONE HUNDRED DOLLARS to 'THE GOLD BUG' . . . written by Edgar Allan Poe, Esq., of this city — and a capital story the committee pronounce it to be."

It was a fitting choice. Rather like the *Dollar Newspaper* itself, "The Gold-Bug" is a crowd-pleaser. The tale of an eccentric South Carolina gentleman who discovers Captain Kidd's buried treasure, it had something for everyone: a pirate story complete with skulls and a treasure chest, an invisible ink cipher, a riddle and a rebus thrown in for good measure, and low racial comedy from a slave who cannot tell his left hand from his right.

Just a few months earlier Poe had complained to a friend, "I have lost, in time, which to me is money, more than a thousand dollars in solving ciphers." But in "The Gold-Bug," the puzzle-solving paid off — for the story centers around a frequency-analysis decryption worthy of one of his *Alexander's Weekly Messenger* columns, and indeed very nearly places some of Poe's own musings as a columnist into the mouths of his characters. Poe's real stroke of genius, adding pirates to a puzzle challenge, may have been inspired by a brief flare of interest in Captain Kidd the year before, after an absurd news story circulated of a woman trying to lay legal claim upon Kidd's treasure by claiming to be his sister. "If this lady really is a sister of Captain Kidd," one newspaper mused, "she must be rather advanced in life by this time, inasmuch as her hopeful brother was duly and properly hanged one hundred and forty-one years ago."

"The Gold-Bug" proved a veritable Kidd's treasure chest itself: within a week of the prize announcement, headlines reported "A GREAT RUSH FOR THE PRIZE STORY!" The *Dollar Newspaper* scrambled to copyright the piece and quickly ran second and third printings. The story's fame only increased when, after one columnist pronounced it "a decided humbug," Poe frivolously threatened to take him to court. The suit never came to pass, but over the next six weeks nearly every other kind of grandstanding did. There was a quick *Graham's* pamphlet cash-in titled "The Prose Romances of Edgar A. Poe, Volume 1"—they never got around to a Volume 2—a hastily mounted stage version by Philadelphia's American Theatre, and a Baltimore store advertising "Gold Bug" lottery tickets, claiming they had a winner who netted a small fortune after dreaming about Poe's story.

By Poe's own estimate, the *Dollar Newspaper* and pirated reprints put 300,000 copies of "The Gold-Bug" into circulation, though the unauthorized reprints did nothing to help Poe's finances. By September, he was reduced to asking the impoverished James Lowell to pay for "The Tell-Tale Heart"—an extremity he'd almost promised not to resort to. He'd already skillfully salvaged the story for a new publication a couple of weeks earlier of "The Black Cat," which reprises the insane first-person narrator of "The Tell-Tale Heart" into a similarly plotted tale of domestic murder. But even that publication, and the five dollars

Lowell scraped together to send to Poe, wasn't nearly enough. Poe would have to turn the success of "The Gold-Bug" toward a new and desperately needed source of income: lecturing.

Education had been changing in the fifteen years since Poe had left the University of Virginia, most notably in the rise of the lyceum movement, an informal circuit of lecture halls that hosted educational lectures by traveling writers and scholars. In an era where college education remained scarce, it was a way for Americans to join intellectual discussions of the day — and, organizers hoped, to keep them out of taverns. One can only guess at Poe's thoughts when he found himself booked into such venues as Temperance Hall; nonetheless, he took to it with gusto, debuting in Philadelphia that November as a speaker on the subject of American poetry. Criticism was a subject he never tired of, after all, even if the advertisements described him as "author of the Gold-Bug, &c." To Poe, that "&c." was above all poetry, and concomitantly the thrashing of bad poetry.

"With the exception of some occasional severity, which however merited, may have appeared too personal, the lecture gave general satisfaction," a Philadelphia newspaper reported that weekend, noting that Poe had particular scorn for logrolling praise by critics for each other's work. "Mr. P laid bare its system of almost universal and indiscriminate eulogy, bestowed alike upon anything and everything — 'from the most elaborate quarto of Noah Webster, down to a penny edition of Tom Thumb.'"

Poe successfully repeated the lecture in other cities, but by the spring of 1844, he'd cycled through many nearby mid-Atlantic venues; going further would take him far from his aunt and his ailing wife, and his disastrous lost week in Washington had already shown him how dangerous that was. Instead, that spring saw Poe revealing to editors what would be the most polished of his detective stories: "The Purloined Letter."

After the creative landmark of "Rue Morgue" and the unexpected dead end of "Marie Roget," Poe's latest story represented a perfecting of the form — a demonstration that the detective story was not only repeatable, but wonderfully adaptable. In telling the story of a devious government minister who hides a stolen document, Poe finally mastered the characters *around* his protagonist of Dupin. Here the police prefect so airily dismissed in "Rue Morgue" becomes that sturdy archetype of the detective genre: the by-the-book police chief. The sidekick, though still unnamed, is at long last given real dialogue — including a questioning of the visiting prefect that shows Dupin and his sidekick developing the easy rapport of a true detective duo:

> "Proceed," said I.
> "Or not," said Dupin.

Poe had learned much from the failed plotting of "Marie Roget" and the successful characterizations of "The Gold-Bug"; now the entire story leads inexorably to the ending, and Dupin only lectures through *some* of it — after the prefect and the sidekick have appeared in scene with him. Poe himself was aware of just what he had achieved. Writing to James Lowell soon afterwards, he admitted that "'The Purloined Letter,' forthcoming in *The Gift*, is, perhaps, the best of my tales of ratiocination."

For what Poe terms *ratiocination* — that is, deductive analysis and puzzle-solving — does indeed remain at the center of "The Purloined Letter." For those who had simply associated Poe's stories with sensational gore and insanity, this was a key revelation. While it was true that "Rue Morgue" featured a double-murder with a victim nearly shoved straight up a chimney, that was not an essential feature of the story. There is no direct violence at all in "The Purloined Letter" — nothing but the faint threat of it, perhaps, and the distraction of a blank pistol fired outside. The action of the story, such as it is, involves shuffling a couple of pieces of paper.

Dupin's deductive process — which, as in "Rue Morgue," the story compares at length to puzzles and gameplay — proves to be one of the most simple and powerful motives in fiction. That motive, curiously, has very little to do with violence or sensation at all. It is the bringing of order to disorder, and causality to the seemingly inexplicable. This is why, whether it features a mere document or a ghastly corpse, mystery readers ever since have associated the genre's classic form with a curious sort of comfort; it is the same satisfaction as in solving a crossword.

Had Poe never written another line, his place in history would still be assured. With "The Purloined Letter," he had demonstrated that the detective story was no fluke, but a wondrously flexible and compelling mode of storytelling — a genre that could grow into one of the most popular forms of literature in the world. And like many authors at the height of their powers, Poe saw where his path would inevitably lead next: New York City.

4

The Shakespeare of America

I T IS NOT OFTEN that we can imagine ourselves in the
place of Edgar Allan Poe, but there is one day we can conjure
rather well: that of April 7, 1844. It was a sleepy morning
in Greenwich Village, with the latest papers reporting "Nothing of the slightest consequence in the legislative proceedings
yesterday"; the only excitement to be found was from the P. T.
Barnum's American Museum & Perpetual Fair a few blocks
over, which advertised "MR. AND MRS. RANDALL, the largest
GIANT! AND GIANTESS!! in the world."

Poe was contentedly recovering from a hearty boarding-
house breakfast—"excellent-flavored coffee, hot & strong—not
very clear & no great deal of cream—veal cutlets, elegant ham
& eggs & nice bread and butter"—as his wife, Virginia, mended
his pants from where he'd caught them on a nail. With some
time to kill, he wrote a letter to his aunt Maria about the won-
drous metropolis; the letter is perhaps the chattiest and warm-
est he ever wrote. It is a glimpse of the man, rather than the icon.

"When we got to the wharf, it was raining hard," he wrote
of their arrival in Manhattan. "I left her on board the boat, after putting the trunks in the Ladies' cabin, and set off to buy
an umbrella and look for a boarding house. I met a man selling
umbrellas, and bought one for 62 cents. Then I went up Greenwich St. and soon found a boarding house. . . . The house is old
& looks buggy—the landlady is a nice chatty old soul. . . . Her
husband is living with her—a fat, good-natured old soul."

He hadn't forgotten the cat, Catterina, they'd left back home — "I wish Kate could see it — she would faint" — and marveled at the cheap rent ("cheapest board I ever knew, taking into consideration the central situation") and mountainous servings of cake provided by the landlady ("no fear of starving here"). It was a promising start for an ambitious writer's great move to New York City, and he cheerily assured his aunt Maria that until they could afford to pay for her to move up to Manhattan and join them, he and Virginia would keep well.

"I feel in excellent spirits, & haven't had a drop to drink," he added.

With Virginia's tuberculosis at bay for the moment ("she has coughed hardly any and had no night sweat"), they set about finding more permanent digs, settling on rooms in a farmhouse near 84th Street and Broadway — an inexpensive rural location, one so remote that two hundred acres of pasture surrounded it. Strolling through the future midtown and uptown of Manhattan, and boyishly paddling a skiff out onto the Hudson River, Poe saw that it would not remain rustic for long.

"I could not look on the magnificent cliffs, and stately trees, which at every moment met my view, without a sigh for their inevitable doom — inevitable and swift," he predicted. "In twenty years, or thirty at farthest, we shall see nothing more romantic than shipping, warehouses, and wharves."

In fact, the Hudson River had already turned busy with treasure hunters. In the wake of the immense popularity of "The Gold-Bug," a salvage crew announced the discovery of Captain Kidd's wreck in thirty feet of water at the bottom of the Hudson. "A spacious diving bell has been procured, suits of sub-marine armor provided for the workmen, and apparatus for digging, scraping, &c., has likewise been prepared," announced one New York newspaper. Some half a million dollars in stock was issued to salvage investors, and though Poe was well aware of the venture, he was too poor to buy a stake in it himself. That was just as well, as the company was run by swindlers; they planted artifacts in the river, "found" them, and ran off with a small fortune from gullible New Yorkers.

Poe, though, already had his own hoax in the works.

"ASTOUNDING NEWS! By Express, via Norfolk! THE AT-LANTIC CROSSED IN THREE DAYS! SIGNAL TRIUMPH OF MR. MONCK MASON'S FLYING MACHINE!!!" roared the front page of the *Sun* on April 13, 1844. By their account, eight Englishmen — including well-known aeronaut Monck Mason and popular author Harrison Ainsworth — had crossed the ocean in an immense airship dubbed *The Victoria*. "The Great Problem is at length solved!" exulted the paper in its lengthy cover story. "The air, as well as the earth and the ocean, has been subdued by science, and will become a common and convenient highway for mankind."

New Yorkers were stunned, but the feat had been a long time in coming. There were claims in New York newspapers as early as 1800 that "A whole fleet of balloons is soon to proceed to America" from France. By 1835, Manhattanites were informed that a balloonist planned to pilot an "Aerial Ship" from downtown Manhattan across the ocean, and in recent months the Pennsylvania balloonist John Wise had announced yet another attempt. Still, news of a successful flight — "unquestionably the most stupendous, the most interesting, and the most important undertaking, ever accomplished or even attempted by man"— excited enough New Yorkers that, at least by Poe's account, "the whole square surrounding the 'Sun' building was literally besieged. . . . I never witnessed more intense excitement to get possession of a newspaper."

It was, of course, a complete humbug.

New Yorkers did not stay duped for long: though Poe's name appears nowhere in the story, having *The Victoria* land at Sullivan's Island was a tip-off, as he'd used the same setting for "The Gold-Bug." But coming just a week after his arrival in the city, the hoax was a fine calling card, even if Poe was slightly irritated to still find himself a footnote to Richard Locke Adams's "Moon Hoax" years earlier in the same paper. "The *success* of the hoax is usually attributed to its correctness," he pointed out afterwards. "The 'Balloon-Story,' which had *no* error, and which related nothing that might not really have happened, was discredited on account of the frequent previous deceptions, of similar character, perpetrated by the *Sun.*"

It was newspapers and magazines, though, where Poe would have to earn his living in New York. For despite his hopes that Charles Dickens would find him a London publisher, none was forthcoming—and nor would there ever be, as they were free to simply pirate American work.

"The want of an International Copy-right Law, by rendering it nearly impossible from the booksellers in the way of remuneration for literary labor, has had the effect of forcing many of our very best writers into the service of Magazines and Reviews," Poe complained in an editorial. Poe certainly had himself in mind; in the autumn of 1844 he'd landed work at the *New York Mirror,* editing copy and writing unsigned items. "It was rather a step downward" from editing *Graham's,* his boss Nathaniel Parker Willis admitted later, but it was the best job they could offer.

Penning pieces with titles like "Try a Mineralized Pavement" was hardly what Poe had foreseen when he moved, though he could take a certain droll amusement in hackwork. Stopping by a tobacco shop one evening, he found employee Gabriel Harrison struggling to pen a campaign song for the local Democratic party, and offered his assistance. "While I was waiting upon a customer," Harrison recalled later, "he had composed a song to the measure and time of the 'The Star-Spangled Banner.'" The hastily penned lyrics ("See the White Eagle soaring aloft to the sky / Wakening the broad welkin with his loud battle cry . . .") suited Harrison fine, though the erstwhile songwriter demurred any payment but "a pound of my best coffee." When the grateful Harrison asked the lyricist for his name, he smiled faintly.

"Thaddeus Perley, at your service," he replied.

It was not until later that Harrison was introduced to the same gentleman under a different name — and by then, there would be few indeed who could not recite a few lines by Edgar Allan Poe.

There was more than mere whimsy to Poe's songwriting; as the child of a theatrical family, music remained one of his most powerful and inchoately recalled loves. "I am profoundly excited by music, and some poems," he wrote that year to James Lowell. "Music is the perfection of the soul, or idea, of Poetry. The vagueness of exaltation aroused by a sweet air (which should be indefinite and never too strongly suggestive) is precisely what we should aim at."

Although his hackwork and fiction paid better, Poe's first love remained poetry. The Romantic bards of his youth — Keats, Byron, Moore, and Coleridge — all possessed a "vagueness of exaltation" exemplified in the latter's dreamlike "Kubla Khan," and a musicality so pronounced that in Moore's case he was initially famed as a balladeer. (Tellingly, Poe was unmoved by the more prosaic Wordsworth.) As a critic, Poe's most extravagant praise went to poets, particularly Alfred Tennyson and Elizabeth Barrett. Drawing upon the meter of the future Mrs. Browning's "Lady Geraldine's Courtship," Poe hit upon the opening lines of his most famous work, "The Raven":

> *Once upon a midnight dreary, while I pondered, weak and*
> *weary,*
> *Over many a quaint and curious volume of forgotten lore —*
> *While I nodded, nearly napping, suddenly there came a*
> *tapping,*

As of some one gently rapping, rapping at my chamber door.
"'Tis some visitor," I muttered, "tapping at my chamber
   door—
      Only this and nothing more."

One question too rarely asked of poems is why they are poems at all; after all, if one were to remove the line breaks and rhymes from the above lines, it would remain unmistakably a work by Poe. Midnight, dreariness, the strategically unnamed old tome, the liminal state of just dropping off to sleep, the denial of a supernatural visitation: we might as easily speak of Ligeia or Roderick Usher. And as it unfolds, the raven driving the grieving narrator mad with refrains of "Nevermore" serves as the same compulsive, self-destructive agent as heartbeats or black cats do for Poe's other increasingly frantic narrators.

But by rendering it as a poem, Poe's favored arc of visitation, denial, and destruction is laid bare in the space of a single newspaper column; both thematically and visually, it has what Poe would later call a "unity of effect." Even a child can spot and then anticipate the cumulative pattern of "The Raven," a powerful repetition inexorably heightening into wild despair; when combined with the easily memorized meter, and a stylized tragic loss without any of the visceral horrors of Poe's fictions, it is a poem that any child or adult *could* read.

Poe knew he had achieved something rare in "The Raven." Unusually for him, he sent a draft to the British poet Richard Horne—whose epic poem "Orion" Poe greatly respected—to ask him his opinion of the work, and to forward it to Elizabeth Barrett. Perhaps Poe already knew what their reaction would be. His friend William Ross Wallace—who himself achieved fame with "The Hand That Rocks the Cradle"—also recalled Poe reading him the still-unpublished lines, to which Wallace replied that they were "fine, uncommonly fine."

"Fine?" Poe scoffed. "Is that all you can say for this poem? I tell you it's the greatest poem ever written."

New York could not have been better prepared for its arrival. "The Purloined Letter" had finally run in *The Gift,* where it attracted some warm notice; and a few weeks later, a new issue of *Graham's* featured a generous profile of Poe by James Russell Lowell, along with an engraved portrait of the author looking oddly placid—hopeful, even. When "The Raven" first appeared in print in the January 29, 1845, issue of the New York *Evening Mirror,* it was the culmination of all that Poe had moved to Manhattan for: a recognition of his genius.

"We are permitted to copy (in advance of publication) from the 2d number of the *American Review,* the following remarkable poem by EDGAR POE," the newspaper's notice by editor N. P. Willis began. "In our opinion, it is the most effective single example of 'fugitive poetry' ever published in this country. . . . It will stick in the memory of everybody who reads it."

Willis was right—more than he or Poe or anyone else could have imagined. "The Raven" sprouted in newspapers across the nation; one fellow poet in New York marveled how "Soon 'The Raven' became known everywhere, and everyone was saying 'Nevermore.'" Perhaps the clearest sign of its currency was parodies appeared ranging from "The Owl" ("But the owl he looked so lonely, saying that word and that only / That a thimble-ful of whiskey I did speedily outpour"), to "The Veto" ("Once upon an evening dreary, the Council pondered weak and weary / Over many a long petition which was voted down a bore"), to a spoof that Abraham Lincoln laughed over titled "The Polecat." Newspaper advertisements promptly took up the idea, and before the season was out an elocution book included the poem among its exercises. "The Raven" was literally a textbook example of American poetry, an honor it has held ever since.

The poem eclipsed even "The Gold-Bug" in popularity—

"the bird beat the bug," Poe mused that spring. But for all its success, it was but a poem: something that always netted less money than fiction, and which brought in nothing at all when pirated. "The Raven" earned Poe even less money than "The Gold-Bug"—just nine dollars, in fact. Yet its fame brought opportunity, for three weeks after "The Raven" appeared, the *Broadway Journal* announced that Poe was joining its masthead as an equal partner. Poe was to furnish one multicolumn page a week to the paper—a perfect bully pulpit.

The critic's pen invariably brought out Poe's worst impulses, most notably a baffling vendetta against the poet Henry Wadsworth Longfellow. Poe had written solicitously to him in the past to seek poems for *Penn* and *Graham's*. But now—first anonymously, and then under his byline—he let fly at a poet who he considered unmusical and "infected with a moral taint," cardinal sins in Poe's view of poetry. And he had a worse accusation: that Longfellow's "Midnight Mass for the Dying Year" was plagiarized from Tennyson.

"[It] belongs to the most barbarous class of literary piracy," Poe insisted, "that class in which, while the words of the wronged author are avoided, his most intangible, and therefore his least defensible and least reclaimable property, is appropriated."

The charge was ludicrous, particularly coming from the sticky-fingered Poe, and Longfellow wisely chose not to respond. But a reader took up Longfellow's defense under the pen name "Outis," and Poe responded at endless length throughout his March 1845 columns. In fact, Outis may well have been Poe himself, and their "argument" a grandstanding monologue. Publisher Charles Briggs privately admitted that "Poe is a monomaniac on the subject of plagiarism," and later added, "Poe's Longfellow war, which, by the way, is all on one side, has annoyed a good deal."

A calculated attack on a respected writer is an old ploy; it quickly yields a splendid borrowed heat and leaves a cold ash of ill will. But for the moment, Poe was hot — and capitalizing upon that meant lecturing. It began well enough; three hundred showed up to hear Poe declaim upon "Poets and Poetry of America," where he dissected the leading poets in Rufus Griswold's recent anthology of the same name, and he inevitably admired and damned Longfellow in equal measure. But when a second lecture scheduled for April 17 fell apart, Poe was caught off-balance.

"It stormed incessantly, with mingled rain and hail and sleet," recalled an office boy from the *Broadway Journal*. "In consequence there were scarcely a dozen persons there, when Poe came upon the platform [to cancel the lecture].... The next morning he came to the office, leaning on the arm of a friend, intoxicated with wine."

It should have been merely a disappointing evening for Poe; instead, it was about to become a disaster.

It is a mark of how serious Poe had been in the literary ambitions of his move to New York that, until that evening, he had stayed sober for over a year, sticking instead to his much happier love of strong coffee. It had served his art well, not least by allowing him to keep a steady day job; in his editorial work he had been, as *Mirror* editor Nathaniel Parker Willis commented, "punctual and industriously reliable."

But now Poe fell back into drinking, and he fell hard. A week after his canceled lecture, a local paper archly announced publication of "A treatise on 'Aqua Pura,' its uses and abuses, by Edgar Allan Poe"; a month later, James Lowell finally met Poe in person, only to find him "tipsy ... & with that oversolemnity with which men in such cases try to convince you of their sobriety." Even that pretense couldn't hold up; Poe canceled a July 1st NYU lecture on account of his being "dreadfully unwell," though his mentor and fellow poet Thomas Chivers found him staggering outside a Nassau Street bar, monumentally drunk and "tottering from side to side," while a bar patron yelled out that he was "the Shakespeare of America."

Poe's literary reputation had indeed never been better. That week brought the release of *Tales,* his first new book since 1839. Selected by publisher Evert Duyckinck, it included all of Poe's detective stories — presented in succession, they take nearly half its pages — plus every major Poe story except for "The Tell-Tale Heart" and "Ligeia." But almost as important was its title page: "WILEY & PUTNAM'S LIBRARY OF AMERICAN BOOKS. NO 11." Designed by Duyckinck to outclass cheap pirated British books, the series would place Poe alongside later entries by Nathaniel Hawthorne, Margaret Fuller, and a promising newcomer named Herman Melville — a mark of both Duyckinck's extraordinarily good taste, and of just how far "The Gold-Bug" and "The Raven" raised the profile of the rest of Poe's work.

It was also a vindication of Poe's move to New York. He lived scarcely a block from Wiley & Putnam's office on Broadway; even when he moved downtown to Amity Lane later that summer, he was only a block from both Margaret Fuller and bookseller John Bartlett. The bookshop's location was fortuitous, as Bartlett invited Poe to author salons — and knew the writing life well enough to pile the table with bread, butter, and coffee. Along with Poe, James Fenimore Cooper and Washington Irving were frequent and even daily customers in his shop, as were poets William Cullen Bryant and William Gilmore Simms.

With the publication of *Tales,* they truly welcomed Poe as one of their own. Fuller praised *Tales* on the front page of the *New York Tribune,* and Simms wondered aloud whether Poe was "too original, perhaps, to be a highly successful writer. The people are not prepared for him yet."

Increasingly, though, it was Poe who was not prepared for the people. His drinking aggravated his *Broadway Journal* partners, with Briggs complaining to James Lowell that "He has some good points, but taken altogether he is badly made up." As if to prove the point, a few weeks later Poe inexplicably turned on Lowell in print, accusing his erstwhile ally and biographer of plagiarism—a bitter absurdity that left Lowell to muse, "I have made Poe my enemy by doing him a service."

That Poe was not entirely unaware of his idiosyncrasies was hinted at in that summer's publication of his story "The Imp of the Perverse." An essay with an almost perfunctory inclusion of a murder plot at the end, its real murder is that by the narrator upon himself. Poe glumly notes acts taken in the "spirit of the *Perverse* ... We perpetrate them merely because we feel we should *not*." More subtly, it is a meditation on losing control to irrational compulsion; fittingly, the essay has perhaps the first published description of a musical earworm—that is, "to be thus annoyed with the ringing in our ears, or rather in our memories, of the burthen of some ordinary song, or some unimpressive snatches from an opera."

Self-awareness, if that is what "Imp" was, does not seem to have helped Poe much. The praise for *Tales* was strong enough that Wiley & Putnam made him the first repeat author in their series by collecting a volume of his poetry; he was invited to read a new poem at the season premiere of the Boston Lyceum in October 1845. But Poe found himself unable to versify; by the time he reached the stage in Boston's Odeon Theatre, he'd stayed sober, but still had no poem ready.

The crowd's patience was exhausted even before Poe opened his mouth, as a previous speaker had droned on for over two hours already. When Poe departed from the advertised poem to give an impromptu twenty-minute speech on American poetry, it drove out many patrons. Among those who stayed were Emily Dickinson's future preceptor Thomas Wentworth Higginson, who recalled how Poe then "abruptly began the recitation of his rather perplexing poem, [and] the audience looked thoroughly mystified." Well they might, for Poe had resorted to a poem that was decidedly not new at all: it was his obscure 1829 farrago "Al Aaraaf." While Higginson was won over by it ("walking back to Cambridge my comrades and I felt that we had been under the spell of some wizard"), the few left by the end were only mollified by a recitation of "The Raven." Boston newspapers did not fondly recall Poe afterwards, and the feeling was mutual.

Returning home, he found the *Broadway Journal* in such dire straits that he bought out his partner for fifty dollars — though even that was borrowed — and promptly used its pages to jeer at his Boston audience. He claimed, not quite convincingly, that the reading was another of his delightful hoaxes, this time on the fools in Boston's literary establishment.

"The Bostonians are well in their way," Poe wrote mockingly. "Their hotels are bad. Their pumpkin pies are delicious. Their poetry is not so good." Just to rub it in, he added that "Al-Aaraaf" was written at the age of ten. After scolding half the Boston audience for rudely leaving during the lecture, he mocked the remainder for being hoaxed by a juvenile production, and "applauding, all those knotty passages which we ourselves have not yet been able to understand."

That did not keep Poe from including "Al Aaraaf" in *The Raven and Other Poems* when it arrived in bookstores several weeks later. While self-deprecation was the norm in prefaces of the time, Poe's went further than most: "I think nothing in this volume of much value to the public," he stated flatly. The claim is only half true; a volume containing "The Raven" and "The Valley of Unrest" is hardly valueless. But to goose the manuscript up to book length, Poe had indeed resorted to larding in juvenilia like "Tamerlane" and "Al Aaraaf" and failed experiments like "Scenes from *Politian*"; he had given so little thought to saving the latter production that he had to borrow back issues of *Southern Literary Messenger* just to transcribe it.

The volume was received politely enough, though with much puzzlement over the juvenilia. Margaret Fuller, as ever, was one of the first out of the gate, with an assertion that "The Raven" alone was a masterpiece, while the other poems showed an unrealized potential—"the productions in this volume indicate a power to do something far better."

Certainly Poe's fiction continued from strength to strength; even as reviews of his poetry came in, the *American Review* carried his minor science fiction hoax "The Facts in the Case of M. Valdemar," a sly account of hypnotic suspended animation that was gullibly reprinted as a fact in both America and Britain. But as gratifying as the poetry reviews and the Valdemar reprints were, Poe had little time to take notice; for over at the *Broadway Journal* offices, his business was taking on water.

It was a cruel irony. After years of trying to start *Penn* and *The Stylus,* living the dream of having his own publication entirely overwhelmed Poe: underfunded and lacking copy, he desperately heaved in book excerpts and uncredited repeats of his own more obscure short stories. A young Walt Whitman visited the office and found Poe "very kindly and human, but subdued, perhaps a little jaded"—and happy to run Whitman's piece on music in the November 29 issue. Poe praised it in print by announcing "we agree with our correspondent throughout," some of the first praise that Whitman received from a major literary figure.

But what Poe needed above all was money. A scant five weeks into his ownership, he sold off half the publication to a partner. Poe drank through the holidays and left the next issue with an entire column blank—the editor's equivalent of giving up on life. By January 3, 1846, his partner had enough and declared the paper over.

That day found Poe at home—two books, one famous poem, and a wrecked magazine away from where he'd been a year earlier. He was famous, jobless, drunk. Musing over a letter that had come in with yet another cryptogram—readers still tormented Poe with them—he turned from the sodden puzzle of his own life to the one on the page before him. As he worked out the cipher, the mocking words emerged: *"And when they wanted wine, the mother of Jesus saith unto him, they have no wine . . ."*

Dispatch boys scurried through Manhattan streets, bearing sacks of valentines — the post office had hired a hundred extra letter carriers just for the day — and Virginia Poe sat up from her sickbed, picked up a pen, and carefully wrote a romantic acrostic poem to her husband:

> *Ever with thee I wish to roam —*
> *Dearest my life is thine.*
> *Give me a cottage for my home*
> *And a rich old cypress vine,*
> *Removed from the world with its sin and care*
> *And the tattling of many tongues.*
> *Love alone shall guide us when we are there —*
> *Love shall heal my weakened lungs;*
> *And Oh, the tranquil hours we'll spend,*
> *Never wishing that others may see!*
> *Perfect ease we'll enjoy, without thinking to lend*
> *Ourselves to the world and its glee —*
> *Ever peaceful and blissful we'll be.*
>   *Saturday, February 14, 1846.*

It is the only surviving note we have from her, and a heartbreakingly earnest and tender one. Amid Edgar's drinking and the loss of his magazine, Virginia's "weakened lungs" had continued their decline. The little family that Edgar had built around his wife and aunt drew ever closer around one another.

They had suffered "tattling tongues" of late, too: a few weeks earlier, after historian Elizabeth Ellet came to regret some unreciprocated letters she sent to Edgar, her quick-tempered brother threatened to thrash the author. Poe drunkenly blundered into the home of his colleague and sometime friend Thomas Dunn English to borrow a pistol to defend himself. When English refused, the two broke into fisticuffs, with Poe getting the worse of it as English socked him across the face with a signet ring; as they were separated, the bloodied Poe sputtered, "Let him alone. I've got him just where I want him."

It was as well that he didn't get the pistol; even drunk, Poe was still one of the few men of letters in his generation with army training. But the whole affair left Poe shunned from that year's Valentine's Day literary salons, and rather joining his wife in longing to leave the downtown "world and its sin and care." Aunt Maria owned a small lot in Baltimore, but was so far behind on taxes that the city announced its seizure. Instead, short of money and good will alike, that May the Poe household moved to the sleepy Bronx suburb of Fordham.

Their new neighborhood was no literary hub; its greatest recent fame was for hosting a field-plowing competition. Fittingly, the approach to Poe's house was, one visitor observed, "half buried with fruit trees." Author Mary Gove Nicholls visited to find a diminutive farmhouse amid a rolling lawn; the cherry groves attracted birds, and Edgar was outside, trying to train a bobolink that he had caught.

"He had put him in a cage, which he had hung on a nail driven into the trunk of a cherry tree," Nicholls mused. "The poor bird was as unfit to live in a cage as his captor was to live in the world."

Yet Poe had left a great many miseries of the city behind, amusing himself with long walks to the woods and to St. John's College, the future Fordham University. He had certainly not traded urban life for more indoor space; his home had just three rooms for as many inhabitants, with a kitchen, a parlor, and an upstairs bedroom crammed under the eaves. To Nicholls — a reform writer on everything from water cures to free love, not long back from visiting Fourierist colonies in the Midwest — the home was simplicity itself, if too spartan even for an idealist like herself.

"So neat, so poor, so unfurnished, and yet so charming a dwelling I never saw," Nicholls recalled. "The sitting-room floor was laid with check matting; four chairs, a light stand, and a hanging bookshelf completed its furniture. There were pretty presentation copies of books on the little shelves, and the Brownings had posts of honor on the stand." When writing, Poe had a table between two windows that he would repair to, and his cat, Catterina, would leap up onto his shoulders and watch.

Poe had not lost all touch with the outside world; with *Tales* and *The Raven and Other Poems* promptly pirated in London, he saw reviews filtering back from abroad. But his most notable appreciation that spring was a *Graham's* essay by Poe himself, "The Philosophy of Composition." In it, Poe claimed to have written "The Raven" through a doggedly logical process that appeared to demonstrate how anyone seeking to write a great poem was fated to write "The Raven."

While obviously rooted in Poe's literary criticism, the more subtle origin of "Philosophy" lay in Poe's cryptogram columns and his detective stories, and their great show made of logical elimination and deduction leading to an inevitable result. Of course a poem's topic must be beauty and death intermixed ("the death, then, of a beautiful woman is, unquestionably, the most poetical topic in the world"); indubitably about one hundred lines is an ideal length ("It is, in fact, 108"); surely only "Nevermore" could work as the poem's refrain ("In fact, it was the very first which presented itself"). If Poe's poker-faced claim of a logical formula for poetry was about as believable as his balloon hoaxes, the essay still admirably summarized his notion of working backwards from a story's conclusion for a "unity of effect," as well as his concept that the fleeting, ineffable state of poetry dictates working within "a distinct limit, as regards length, to all works of literary art — the limit of a single sitting."

"The Philosophy of Composition" occasioned little comment that spring, but his absence from downtown did. Newspaper rumors began that he was committed to the Insane Retreat at Utica. He wasn't, but it only fueled curiosity over the announcement by *Godey's Magazine* days later that Poe was to write a series of profiles on "The Literati of New York City." Featuring bewilderingly frank descriptions of New York editors and authors, its May 1846 issue quickly sold out. Amid Poe's usual mingled praise and stabbing criticism, startling personal descriptions revealed his old business partner Charles Briggs as "not a person to be disliked, though very apt to irritate and annoy" while he "pretends to a knowledge of French"; the travel writer William Gillespie "walks irregularly, mutters to himself"; of N. P. Willis, Poe judged: "His face is somewhat too full, or rather heavy ... neither his nose nor his forehead can be defended."

Willis, mind you, was a *friend* of his.

Poe had been led terribly astray — for while he was not averse to settling old scores, many of the most tactless descriptions in his profiles originated in a belief in phrenology. Clinical descriptions of weak faces and eccentric mannerisms seem to have been just that to him: descriptions falling within the scientific realm. To anyone else, they were monumental insults. It was, one sympathetic newspaper editor warned, "the maddest kind of honesty." Before the summer was out, Poe's series had goaded his old sparring partner Thomas Dunn English into revealing their fight and Poe's alcoholism to New York newspapers, with Dunn claiming that "a merchant of this city had accused [Poe] of committing forgery." Infuriated by the charge, Poe sued for libel.

Clearly, matters had gotten out of hand. Fellow Southern writer William Gilmore Simms pleaded with Poe: "Suffer me to tell you frankly, taking the privilege of a true friend, that you are now perhaps in the most perilous period of your career." The series was cut short in October, but the damage was done. Thomas Dunn English published a satire of Poe as "Marmaduke Hammerhead," the drunk and impoverished critic and author of "The Black Crow":

> "Did—did—did you ever read my review of L—L—Longfellow?"
> "No!" said the one addressed—a quiet, sober looking personage, "I dare say it's very severe; but I never read it."
> "Well," said Hammerhead, "you lost a gr—gr—eat pleasure. You're an ass!"

If anything good came of their quarrel, it might be the November 1846 publication in *Godey's* of Poe's thinly veiled revenge fantasy, "The Cask of Amontillado"—a dark-humored masterpiece of reverse psychology and ironic dialogue, with its narrator gently leading his victim deeper into a fatal catacomb while insisting that he go no further. Like much of Poe's gothic work, the story's exact time and place are unclear, while the narrator is in sharp focus: it is the disconcertingly sane voice of someone recounting an insane act of murder. It is the victim's pleas for mercy—beseeching, then crazed, then unsettlingly pensive—that are the key to the story being more than merely a masterly tale of sensation. When the narrator evinces the faintest hint of regret at the end, it is with the devastating sense that such glimmers of conscience are simply not enough; there can be no moral to his story, for he is not particularly sorry at all.

Run in lieu of Poe's next set of profiles, "The Cask of Amontillado" certainly did his reputation far more good than a new set of insultingly honest sketches. But instead of continuing to write fiction, Poe struggled with illness and squandered much

of the rest of 1846 on a projected volume of profiles to be titled *Literary America: Some Honest Opinion about our Authorial Merits and Demerits with Occasional Words of Personality.*

"I might make a hit and some profit, as well as proper fame,
by extending the plan into that of a book on American letters
generally, and keeping the publication in my own hands," Poe
explained to a friend. "I am now *at* this—body & soul."

It was a hopeless scheme; Poe lacked the funds to print it
himself, and no sane publisher would acquire a book certain to
anger half of their colleagues in the city. When visitors came to
Poe's farmhouse that December, they found a family shivering,
ill, and without money—and for one of them, with time itself
about to run out.

Amid the usual appeals for the poor that Christmas season, the
December 15, 1846, issue of the New York *Morning Express* had
a particularly surprising one:

> ILLNESS OF EDGAR A. POE—We regret to learn that this
> gentleman and his wife are both dangerously ill with the con-
> sumption, and that the hand of misfortune lies heavy upon
> their temporal affairs. We are sorry to mention the fact that
> they are so far reduced as to be barely able to obtain the ne-
> cessities of life...

The report was quickly picked up by other newspapers across
the country—"Great God!" editorialized the *Bostonian* on
Christmas Eve, "Is it possible, that the literary people of the
Union, will let poor Poe perish by starvation and lean-faced
beggary in New York?" Several editors loudly took up collections. Poe was mortified by the attention, if quietly grateful for
the modest but desperately needed donations that poured in.

"That my wife is ill, then, is true," he admitted to N. P. Willis. Poe's drinking, though, had proven nearly as devastating in the last year: "That I myself have been long and dangerously ill, and that my illness has been a understood thing among my brethren in the press, the best evidence is afforded by the innumerable paragraphs of personal and literary abuse with which I have been latterly assailed. This matter, however, will remedy itself. . . . I am getting better."

Poe had indeed sobered up and was throwing himself into his *Literary America* project. But, always just a room away in their little cottage, Virginia Poe was suffering every bit as badly as the editorials had claimed. A visitor found the household struggling even to keep her sickbed warm; Edgar held and rubbed her hands, Aunt Maria held her feet, and piled atop her was a thin blanket — Edgar's old army overcoat — and Catterina the cat. Donated blankets and pillows soon arrived from friends, but Virginia's condition remained beyond help. In late January 1847, their family friend and nurse Marie Louise Shew received a dire message from Aunt Maria: "But come — oh do come to-morrow!"

She found Virginia propped up in an armchair in the last flush of her sufferings at the age of twenty-four — and desperately concerned that Edgar wasn't left a lonely widower. Virginia grabbed his hand and Marie's and pressed them together. "Marie, be a friend to Eddie, and don't forsake him," she pleaded. "He always loved you — didn't you, Eddie?"

One day later, Virginia was dead. The family's landlord was so touched by their plight that, to keep Virginia from a pauper's grave, he offered space in his own family crypt — and the Poes were so poor that they took it.

Edgar was nearly despaired of as well; his recently regained health fell apart. "He did not seem to care," one acquaintance recalled, "after she was gone, whether he lived an hour, a day, a week or a year; she was his all." At one point he fell senseless and had to be carried to a doctor; when he regained consciousness, he feverishly babbled to his nurse about his long-dead brother Henry—"He talked to me *incessantly,* of the past," she recalled, " ... [and] begged me to write for him his fancies, for he said he had promised so many greedy publishers his next efforts."

Poe awoke from the haze of illness and depression that spring to find his prospects improbably brightened. Though he'd been too sick to attend the court hearings, he'd prevailed in his libel suit, and was awarded over two hundred dollars. Rufus Griswold had deigned to recognize his work in his newly published *Prose Writers of America,* declaring in particular of his mysteries that "a subtle power of analysis is his distinguishing characteristic." Better still, "The Murders in the Rue Morgue" had received the highest possible compliment in Paris: it was translated and passed off by a Frenchman as his own. When the real authorship of "Rue Morgue" was discovered—an impeccable Parisian mystery, by an American!—Poe's reputation rose higher there than perhaps in his own country.

"[Poe] is pestered and annoyed at home by penny-a-liners whom his iron pen has cut into too deeply ..." his editor Evert Duyckinck mused. "It is curious to contrast this with his position abroad, where distance suffers only the prominent features of his genius to be visible."

Visiting for a tea party that June, Duyckinck found Poe recovered and enjoying "the purity of the air" outside; inside, there was a new rug on the floor, and Aunt Maria had laid an improbably decent spread on the table, complete with a new silver-plated coffeepot—the pleasant spoils of his libel suit.

Poe, however, had not quite recovered the strength to write—and what little he did set down that year was salvaged from older work, haunted by an almost paralyzing sense of mourning. His one major poem in 1847, "Ulalume," is effectively an ululation for the dead, and weird and obscure in its effect. It is his most daring work of poetry, adopting insistent repetition to an unnerving effect — not the simple one-word refrain of "The Raven," but the sickbed delirium of entire phrases echoing and twisting from one line to the next:

> *The skies they were ashen and sober;*
> *The leaves they were crisped and sere —*
> *The leaves they were withering and sere:*
> *It was night, in the lonesome October*
> *Of my most immemorial year. . . .*

Poe had likely drafted it the year before — and the first friends and acquaintances to read it were so puzzled by the production that they hardly knew what to make of it.

For his one major prose work of 1847, Poe dug back even further, appending and retitling an obscure 1842 piece. "The Domain of Arnheim" is a curiously moving short story, though. Beginning from the notion of an heir reaping an improbably gigantic bequest after a century of compound interest, the impoverished Poe imagined this poignant question: even if you are the richest man in existence, how can you find happiness? In Poe's earlier story, the heir settles upon landscaping an almost Edenic refuge; but in "Arnheim," the newly added closing scenes follow a boat entering the completed paradise:

> There is a gush of entrancing melody; there is an oppressive sense of strange sweet odor; — there is a dream-like intermingling to the eye of tall slender Eastern trees — bosky shrubberies — flocks of golden and crimson birds — lily-fringed lakes — meadows of violets, tulips, poppies, hyacinths and tuberoses — long intertangled lines of silver streamlets — and, upspringing confusedly from amid all, a mass of semi-Gothic, semi-Saracenic architecture, sustaining itself by miracle in mid-air, glittering in the red sunlight with a hundred oriels, minarets,

and pinnacles; and seeming the phantom handiwork, con-
jointly, of the Sylphs, of the Fairies, of the Genii, and of the
Gnomes.

It bears the haunting pathos of a grieving man imagining an afterlife — and, he admitted privately, the story "expresses much
of my soul."

His musings upon paradise were not exactly theological, as
Poe had never found much solace in church — "The Bible, he
says, is all rigmarole," a scandalized *Broadway Journal* colleague
once reported. But as 1847 came to a close and a new year began,
Poe could often be found late at night standing on the porch of
his cottage and staring at the stars twinkling in the frigid winter air — wondering not just what heaven meant, but what the
heavens signified. He gulped down coffee and excitably kept his
long-suffering aunt up late into the night, warding off solitude
as he set his ideas down to paper.

"He never liked to be alone," she later recalled, "and I used
to sit up with him, often until four o'clock in the morning, he
at his desk, writing, and I dozing in my chair. When he was
composing 'Eureka,' we used to walk up and down the garden,
his arm around mine, until I was so tired I could not walk. He
would stop every few minutes and explain his ideas to me, and
ask if I understood him."

She was likely bewildered by his talk, but Poe had never felt
so sure of himself.

"What I have propounded will (in good time) revolutionize
the world of Physical & Metaphysical Science," Poe wrote to a
friend that February. "I say this calmly — but I say it."

5

Nevermore

I N THE FEBRUARY 3, 1848, issue of the *New York Tribune,* an enigmatic notice was wedged between ads for a "Whig Newspaper Establishment for Sale" and a lecture on "Mesmerism, Somnambulism, Clairvoyance and Hallucination":

> ☞ Edgar A. Poe will lecture at the Society Library on Thursday evening, the 3d inst. at half-past 7. Subject, "The Universe." Tickets 50 cents — to be had at the door

It was a three-line ad, the smallest and cheapest Poe could buy in the *Tribune;* to make it fit, the period at the end was cut off.

Curious readers arrived at the corner of Broadway and Leonard, stepped inside the grand Ionic-columned edifice of the Society Library, and made their way back to one of the lecture rooms. Among those waiting attentively were Poe's old editor Evert Duyckinck and a smattering of newspaper reporters. But more noticeable was who wasn't there: with only about sixty people in the crowd, most of the seats in the hall sat empty.

A thin and pale Edgar Allan Poe took the stage, dressed in his usual black and with his coat tightly buttoned. His subject that evening, he announced, was the very nature of matter itself — the stars, the planets, gravitation and electricity, the beginning and end of the universe — and also, God. Poe began by reciting a droll satire, a letter from the year 2848, from a time

of 300 mph railroads, airships, and "floating telegraph wires"—
and then, quite as unexpectedly, he launched back into cosmol-
ogy. As rain pelted outside and the clock passed nine, his lis-
teners shifted uncomfortably in their seats. Poe, still pondering
gravity and nebular theories, showed no sign of letting up.

"Every minute after that seemed to be possessed of the famous property so conspicuous in his discourse, called gravity,"
one attendee recalled. "It weighed upon the heart. Still no end
was visible; the thin leaves, one after another, of the neat manuscript, were gracefully turned over; yet, oh, plenty more were
left evidently behind."

It was nearly ten by the time the author finished and announced that he wished to raise funds for launching his beloved
Stylus magazine; audience members quietly fled before he could
raise the one hundred dollars he had been hoping for.

"A mountainous piece of absurdity for a popular lecture," an
appalled Duyckinck wrote to his brother afterwards. "It drove
people from the room, instead of calling in subscribers." Newspapers were largely as puzzled or as dismissive as Duyckinck;
the one lengthy and appreciative account of the evening rued
that bad weather kept the crowds away. It was a charitable interpretation, considering the Park Theatre played to a full house
that same night.

The blame was entirely Poe's. The Society Library had
proved hospitable to events by everyone from mesmerists
to Swedenborgian lecturers; the following week, one Signor
Spinetto used it for an exhibition of his "Learned Canary
Birds." But Poe was an author with no new published work
announced for the lecture—the letter from the year 2848 was
from his newly drafted short story "Mellonta Tauta," but he
didn't mention the fact—and he was lecturing on a topic out
of his usual expertise. He'd waited until the last minute to ad-
vertise and barely bought any space in the papers for it. For the

same fifty-cent admission, New Yorkers could go to John Banvard's "Three Mile Painting" that night, or spend half as much on the Christy Minstrels, "the Napoleons of Negro minstrelry." More to the point, they only needed to wait one more night to hear an actual astronomer talk on the recent discovery of Neptune.

Yet Poe remained convinced of his lecture's importance. He made an appointment with publisher George Putnam, and commenced the meeting by staring at him in dead silence for a full minute.

"I am Mr. Poe," he finally said. Putnam was used to eccentric authors, and he knew perfectly well who Poe was.

"I hardly know," Poe continued, "how to begin what I have to say. It is a matter of profound importance."

The author almost trembled with emotion — for, Putnam recalled, "the publication he had to propose was of momentous interest. . . . An edition of fifty thousand copies might be sufficient to begin with, but it would be a small beginning. No other scientific event in the history of the world approached in importance the original developments of this book. All this and more, not in irony or in jest, but in *intense* earnest."

Putnam agreed to publish *Eureka: A Prose Poem*, but the July 1848 print run was not 50,000, but 500. Its few readers opened it to find Poe's most eccentric and puzzling work: "I design to speak of the *Physical, Metaphysical and Mathematical*," he wrote, "— *of the Material and Spiritual Universe — of its Evidence, its Origin, and Creation, its Present Condition and its Destiny.*"

What follows certainly explains his lecture audience's confusion. For the next 143 pages, without chapter or section breaks, Poe argues that the universe emanated from nothingness, spread out from a "Primordial Particle," and that this creative event entailed both forces of attraction (gravity) and repulsion (electricity). Attractive force would eventually collapse the universe upon itself into its original Unity. The deity embodied within this Unity is unknowable by human minds, except through its manifestation in the works of the universe — which, for a critic fond of knocking the Transcendentalists, sounded rather Emersonian.

But Poe went further: what if this process repeated, he asked, so that each expansion and contraction manifested its own God?

"I myself feel impelled to the fancy — without daring to call it more," Poe mused, "that there *does* exist a *limitless* succession of Universes, more or less similar to that of which we cognizance — to that of which *alone* we shall ever have cognizance — at the very least until the return of our Universe into Unity. . . . Each exists, apart and independently, in the bosom of its particular and proper God."

The idea of matter from nothingness could already be found in textbooks, and notions of multiple universes dated back to the ancient Greeks; still, Poe's particular fusion of the ideas has a pleasing oracularity, especially under his poetic talents. Anyone reading of "a novel Universe swelling into existence, and then subsiding into nothingness, at every throb of the Heart Divine" could see the mind behind "Ulalume" at work. Yet this "prose poem" was not a poem in any formal sense; and as prose, Poe gave no particular means of proving his theory beyond intuition, and a smattering of planetary and orbital calculations that one astrophysicist later briskly characterized as "all nonsense" and "numerology."

Eureka's inconsistent narrative voice — sometimes satirical and ludicrous, then pedantic, then stirring and expansive — hearkened back to Poe's early and less confident writing. It was the work of a lonely widower in a remote farmhouse, with neither a spouse nor a magazine editor to contradict him or to keep the work's flaws in check. Poe himself seemed unsure of how to explain the result.

"I offer this book of Truths, not in its character of Truth-Teller, but for the Beauty that abounds in Truth," his preface states. The book is "an Art Product alone"—and yet he emphatically states, "What I here propound is true," before finally allowing that "Nevertheless it is as a Poem only that I wish this work to be judged after I am dead."

In fact, *Eureka*'s genre is quite recognizable: it is crank literature. Any reader of such nineteenth-century panaceas as phrenology, octagonal homes, hollow-earth theory, or Fourierist colonies will find a delightful familiarity in *Eureka*. Such works are typically written by a non-expert, particularly one accustomed to being clever in a different field; with only superficial understanding of their subject, and indeed of scientific method, they may employ false analogies and supposition to make grand, unifying claims on politics, health, religion, and the universe itself. What is bewitching about crank literature is that it may have the kernel of a good idea, a passing observation that seems prophetic. Phrenology hit upon localized brain function and neural plasticity; crusades for octagonal homes posited open planning and concrete construction; even hollow-earth theories served to encourage early expeditions to the Antarctic. That Poe made a glancing proto-evolutionary reference, and a half-right explanation of the darkness of the night sky, did not make *Eureka* scientifically influential; it made it part of a long literary tradition of wildly unproveable near misses.

Reviews of *Eureka* were muted, respectful, and dismissive in equal measure; it is unlikely that Poe earned anything beyond the fourteen dollars that Putnam advanced him, less than he earned on some articles. He had another problem, too: after a stretch of sobriety and a sense of purpose in writing *Eureka,* he was at loose ends. Poe inexorably returned to the dream of his own magazine.

"I am resolved to be my own publisher," he complained to a friend. "To be controlled is to be ruined."

In the summer of 1848, he set off to his old hometown to try once again at raising funds for *The Stylus.* "I am desperately circumstanced — in very bitter distress of mind and body," he explained to a prominent subscriber. "My last hope of extricating myself from the difficulties which are pressing me to death, is in going personally to a distant connection near Richmond."

The trip was a disaster; though he made the rounds and introduced himself to *Southern Literary Messenger* editor John Thompson, he collapsed into drinking. "He remained here about 3 weeks, horribly drunk and discoursing 'Eureka' every night to the audiences of the Bar Rooms," Thompson reported after Poe was bundled back to New York City.

The comment is a telling one. Thompson found Poe unable to write anything else while he visited; the author perseverated on *Eureka,* which he plainly regarded as his magnum opus. As to why Poe felt such an overwhelming connection to the work — declaiming it to any stranger who would listen — one must read its last words, a footnote regarding the collapse of the universe to its original unity:

> *Note — The pain of the consideration that we shall lose our individual identity, ceases at once when we further reflect that the process, as above described, is, neither more nor less than that of absorption, by each individual intelligence, of all other intelligences (that is, of the Universe) into its own. That God may be all in all, *each* must become God.

Virginia Poe had scarcely been in the grave for a year when Poe wrote this. For a man who had spent much of his career touching upon the mysteries of dissolution — of liminal states of death in life, of its phantasmal effect upon the living, of its visceral horrors — *Eureka* was a sincere effort to explain the inexplicable, to face the subject without artifice. That he failed by most measures says less about Poe than about death itself, and how it can leave even a great author at a loss for words.

In Poe's own eyes, though, his work had succeeded. For now he had reconciled himself to death — perhaps too well.

On November 4, 1848, Edgar Allan Poe decided it was time to kill himself. It was a crisp and cold Saturday morning in Providence; after a sleepless night in a hotel room, the author took a brisk walk to clear his mind. The stroll didn't work — "the demon tormented me still," he complained — but it did take him past a pharmacy, and that gave him a fine idea. He bought a powerful enough dose of opium tincture to kill most men, boarded a railway car to Boston without bothering to return to his hotel, and proceeded to write a suicide note. Then, upon reaching the city of his birth, he downed an ounce of the laudanum and walked to the post office with his dying words in hand.

He never made it.

"Before I reached the Post Office my reason was entirely gone, & the letter was never put in," he later wrote dejectedly. "The laudanum was rejected from the stomach, I became calm, & to a casual observer, sane — so that I was suffered to go back to Providence."

It was there that a few days later he was coaxed into sitting for a photograph. The 1848 "Ultima Thule" daguerreotype is today one of the iconic images of the nineteenth century: Poe, staring out into an unreachable middle distance, looking faintly chagrined at his dubious good fortune in having survived.

He was not supposed to be alone and forlorn like this. But Virginia's hope that Poe might marry her deathbed nurse, Marie Shew, had gone awry; their rather simple friend was fond of Poe but piously frightened by *Eureka*. Poe instead conceived a fascination with one the most prominent critics and poets in America, Sarah Helen Whitman. She bore no relation to the still-obscure Walt, but — of far more interest to Poe — she *was* the wealthy widow of a Providence attorney. After quietly finding through a mutual friend that she admired his work, Poe sent a letter under a false name to determine whether she was in Providence at the moment:

> Dear Madam —
>   Being engaged in making a collection of autographs of the most distinguished American authors, I am, of course, anxious to procure your own, and if you would so far honor me as to reply, however briefly, to this note, I would take it as a *very especial* favor.
>
> > Resy Yr mo. ob. st,
> > Edward S. T. Grey

A few weeks later, he contrived to meet her while in town, and in seeking to charm her met with an almost wildly improbable stroke of luck. Visiting the Athenaeum library, she idly asked him about an unsigned poem she'd admired in the *American Review* a year earlier. Had he seen it too? It was called . . . "Ulalume."

"To my infinite surprise," she recalled, "he told me that he himself was the author. Turning to a bound volume of the *Review* which was in the alcove where we were sitting, he wrote his name at the bottom."

This was a sign, surely: and one day later, as they strolled through a local cemetery, Poe asked for her hand in marriage.

It was not quite a perfect match. Whitman's friends included a number of writers whom Poe disliked, and she lived with a fiercely protective mother. Undeterred, Poe tried to overwhelm Helen's doubts with torrential love letters — "Were I not poor — had not my late errors and reckless excesses justly lowered me in the esteem of the good — were I wealthy, or could I offer you worldly honors — ah then — then — how proud I would be to persevere — to sue — to plead — to kneel — to pray — to beseech you for your love — in the deepest humility — at your feet . . ."

Yet Poe still nursed affections for several other women, all with the miserable knowledge that none of them were Virginia. His despair over these lonely courtships was enough that he had simply tried to end it all in Boston. But the widower's pleas to Helen Whitman did not go unheard; at the end of November, she said yes, and they planned a Christmastime marriage. Now it was their friends and her mother who turned dubious. "She has seemed to me a good girl, and — you know what Poe is," editor Horace Greely fretted to his colleague Rufus Griswold. "Has Mrs. Whitman no friend within your knowledge that can faithfully *explain* Poe to her?"

The widow did not have to wait long to find out for herself. Three days before the wedding, Poe's prospective mother-in-law demanded that Poe cut himself out of the Whitman family finances, and promise to stop drinking. He duly agreed, and steeled himself to the task the next morning with some wine at the hotel bar. Within hours the wedding was off — forever.

Poe instead ushered in 1849 half-relieved to not be married, half-dismayed to be unmarried, and altogether worried about his career. Toiling over *Eureka* and futile love letters had come at the expense of paid work; he'd earned $166 in the previous year, barely enough to cover his rent, let alone anything else. "I am about to bestir myself in the world of Letters rather more busily than I have done for three or four years past," he promised an editor.

The unlikely vehicle for this comeback was the *Flag of the Union,* an illustrated Boston weekly relaunching as "a paper for the million." Its wide circulation was not matched by critical regard. "Why do you write for that cheap-literature broad sheet?" one of Poe's friends asked bluntly — "Does the publisher pay you well?" In fact, they did, and contemporaries like Frances Osgood and Lydia Sigourney also wrote for the *Flag*. But as Poe admitted, their fine literary sensibilities were lost on the venue: "whatever I send it I feel I am consigning to the tomb of the Capulets."

Still, the *Flag*'s need to fill columns coaxed Poe into his most productive period since the collapse of the *Broadway Journal;* between February and June of 1849, he published as many new pieces of fiction as in the previous four years combined. "Literature is the most noble of professions. In fact, it is about the only one fit for a man," he now declared amid reports of the Gold Rush. "Nor would I abandon all the hopes which lead me on for all the gold in California."

Amid a number of trifles that he sent to the *Flag of the Union,* his revenge tale "Hop-Frog" showed Poe in fine form. Set in the indistinct time and place favored by his gothic fiction, it continues the theme of alcohol-fueled rage and cold-blooded murder from "The Black Cat" and "The Cask of Amontillado," this time through the horrifying vengeance upon a king and his councilors by a court dwarf. Maddened by forced draughts of wine, he traps his tormentors into donning flammable costumes made of tar and flax, and exults over their "fetid, blackened, hideous, and indistinguishable mass" as he escapes through a skylight: "I am simply Hop-Frog, the jester — and *this is my last jest.*"

It was very nearly Poe's as well: after the *Flag of the Union* quietly sent letters to contributors announcing that it could no longer pay for articles, the false spring of Poe's output was over. He turned back to his fondest mirage: his own magazine, so that he might not be tormented by these unreliable editors. His hopes were unexpectedly stoked by a timely letter from a young prospective investor, one Edward Horton Norton Patterson. There was just one catch: Patterson wanted to headquarter this new national literary powerhouse in his unprepossessing hometown of Oquawka, Illinois ... and instead of *The Stylus*, he wanted the title to be the *Oquawka Spectator.*

"Some serious difficulties present themselves ..." Poe suggested tactfully. "Your residence at Oquawka is certainly one of the most serious." But Patterson was the most solid backer he'd seen in years, and Poe set off to tour the East Coast to gather subscriptions, despite his aunt Maria fretting over his health.

"Do not fear for Eddie!" he called to her as he left.

Days later, in the Philadelphia engraving room of magazine editor John Sartain, Poe burst in, looking wild and begging to be hidden. "It would be difficult for you to believe what I have to tell—that such things could be in the nineteenth century," he babbled. "It is necessary that I remain concealed for a time. Can I stay here with you?" He'd been riding on a train, Poe explained, and heard men several seats back plotting to kill him.

"If this moustache of mine were removed I should not be so readily recognized," he proposed. "Will you lend me a razor, that I may shave it off?"

Sartain played along, and finally coaxed the shorn author to stroll the streets and sit by the reservoir. Slowly a different story emerged. Poe had been in the local Moyamensing prison, where he'd seen a boiling cauldron and witnessed his aunt Maria having her legs sawn off—first "her feet, then her legs at the knee, her thighs at the hips, and so destroy her piecemeal, all to torture me." Poe calmly related these hallucinations as facts. He also claimed he'd been jailed for a counterfeit fifty-dollar note. But the prison stay, Sartain suspected, was for drunkenness. It had only been a few hours, for he was recognized in the courtroom—"Why, this is Poe the poet," they said—and then let go.

The hallucinations may have been delirium tremens—for at forty, Poe's body was finally beginning to rebel. When he turned up a week later at the door of his fellow gothic novelist George Lippard, he was in even worse shape—wandering penniless through a local cholera epidemic, starving and wearing only one shoe. Poe collapsed into a corner of Lippard's office, his head in his hands.

"It is no use to reason with me now; I must die," he wrote back home in a despairing letter to his aunt Maria. "I have no reason to live since I have done *Eureka*."

Lippard did his best to console him — feeding and clothing him, getting fellow writers to pitch in train fare to continue his journey. But when he helped Poe board the southbound night train, Lippard sensed something different in his old friend. "He held our hand for a long time, and seemed loth to leave us," he recalled, "— there was in his voice, look and manner, something of a Presentiment that his strange and stormy life was near its close."

The trip back to his childhood home of Richmond began wretchedly: he was heading into a Southern summer still dressed in the miserable black clothing that he'd worn in jail. "My clothes are *so horrible,* and I am *so ill,*" he wrote to his aunt Maria as he neared Richmond. Worse still, his poetry lectures, with which he'd hoped to raise money while on the road, had disappeared from his valise in Philadelphia: "All the object of my trip here is over unless I can recover them or rewrite one of them," he lamented.

But his arrival in Richmond, with just two dollars left in his pocket, was followed by a desperately needed reprieve: a fifty-dollar check from his Oquawkan benefactor. Poe cleaned up, bought himself a jaunty summer hat, and went looking for his college girlfriend. Not only was Elmira Royster still in Richmond, she had been widowed with an estate of some $100,000. She was busying herself for church one Sunday morning when, she recalled, "a servant told me that a gentleman in the parlour wanted to see me." She went downstairs and recognized him instantly.

"Oh! Elmira, is this you?" he called out.

She would not be kept from going to church, but when he came back again later, his mind was already made up: he thought they should get married. "I laughed at it . . ." she admitted. "Then I found he was serious and I became serious."

He became serious enough to tell a doctor that he'd stop drinking; serious enough to rewrite his lecture on "The Poetic Principle" and announce it for a local concert venue. Poe lectured a packed house; topped off with a crowd-pleasing recitation of "The Raven," it was a sort of calling card to Richmond society. Their poet had come back home, and for his encore, he delivered a stunning surprise: on August 27, 1849, he joined the local chapter of the Sons of Temperance. Poe had become a very serious suitor indeed. When he delivered a second lecture to Richmond the next month, Mrs. Royster could be seen sitting together in the front row, watching his performance of "The Raven" and his recitations from memory of Byron, Tennyson, and — yes, even Longfellow.

September was improbably happy for Poe — the best weeks of his life, he said, though of the bittersweet sort that suited him best. He was literally trailed by his past; his little sister, Rosalie Poe, still in Richmond after being raised by a different family, now so devotedly followed him around that he took to sending her out on errands. He visited old childhood friends, surprising them with his sobriety; rambling with them through the ruins of a neighborhood home from his youth, Poe sat down on the moss-covered remains of an old bench.

"There used to be white violets here," he muttered, and then walked inside the wrecked house. He paused out of sheer habit, one friend recalled, to politely remove his hat as he entered the destroyed parlor. Other memories flooded back to him at strange, unexpected places. Invited to address a small assembly in Norfolk, he seemed momentarily stunned by one woman's orris root perfume.

"Do you know what it makes me think of?" he asked her.

"My adopted mother. Whenever the bureau drawers of her room were opened there was the whiff of orris root, and ever since, when I smell it, I go back to the time when I was a little boy."

By the end of September, it was rumored that Poe and Elmira were engaged, and at the very least they had reached a cautious understanding; first, though, business was to call him away. There was still *The Stylus* to consider, and his aunt Maria in New York to consult about the nuptials; he had also landed a lucrative offer of one hundred dollars to stop off in Philadelphia to edit the poems of a piano manufacturer's wife. So he bade a melancholy farewell to Elmira—"He was very sad, and complained of being quite sick," she recalled—stopped by a doctor's office, and then took a steamer from the Richmond docks in the small hours of September 27.

Nobody is quite sure what happened next. On October 3rd, Dr. Joseph Snodgrass, a Baltimore literary friend of Poe's who had been the first to publish "Ligeia" a decade earlier, received this urgent note:

Baltimore City, Oct. 3, 1849

There is a gentleman, rather worse for the wear, at Ryan's 4th ward polls, who goes under the cognomen Edgar A. Poe, and who appears in great distress, & says he is acquainted with you, and I assure you, he is in need of immediate assistance.

Yours, in haste,
Jos. W. Walker

Snodgrass raced over to a nearby saloon and found Poe glassy-eyed and semiconscious—"utterly stupefied with liquor"—and in his oblivion his clothing had been robbed or pawned and replaced by a thin and soiled outfit. It had been rainy and in the fifties that weekend, and "the atmosphere partook sensibly of a spongy character" as one local put it; Poe might well have also have suffered from exposure. Refused help by Poe's local relatives, Snodgrass checked him in to Washington College Hospital. "So insensible was he," he wrote, "that we had to carry him to the carriage as if a corpse."

At 3 A.M. on October 5, Poe trembled violently, his body drenched in sweat; when he came to the following afternoon, his doctor could get little coherent from him except the half-right notion that he "had a wife in Richmond." Dr. John Moran told his delirious patient that soon he might recover to see his family and friends.

"At this he broke out with much energy," Dr. Moran reported, "and said the best thing his best friend could do would be to blow his brains out with a pistol."

For the next two days, Poe alternated between uneasy dozing and such violent delirium that two nurses had to restrain him. On Saturday evening, Dr. Moran reported, "he commenced calling for one 'Reynolds,' which he did through the night up to *three* on Sunday morning." Reynolds might have been the polar explorer Jeremiah Reynolds, whom Poe had drawn upon for *The Narrative of Arthur Gordon Pym* — and whose hollow-earth theories ventured that Antarctica might hold the portal to a hidden realm.

It was an apt invocation for a guide to the underworld. At five that morning, Edgar Allan Poe met the fate anticipated in his poem "To Annie":

> *Thank Heaven! the crisis —*
> *The danger is past,*
> *And the lingering illness,*
> *Is over at last —*
> *And the Fever called 'Living'*
> *Is conquer'd at last.*

He was buried the following afternoon with scarcely a dozen people in attendance, and that included the undertakers. One witness scoffed that the ceremony "did not occupy more than three minutes, [and] was so cold-blooded and un-Christianlike as to provoke on my part a sense of anger." When it was over, his body was left in an unmarked grave.

Word of Poe's death spread quickly. On the morning of his funeral, the *Baltimore Sun* failed to announce the service, but mourned that his death "will cause poignant regret among all who admire genius, and have sympathy for the frailties too often attending it." By the following day similar reports had run up the coast to New York. Even the harshest obituary, in the *New York Herald*—"he had few or no friends," it claimed—acknowledged that Poe was a genius, with speech "almost supramortal in its eloquence," and invested with a grandly Romantic persona: "He was at all times a dreamer—dwelling in ideal realms—in heaven or hell—peopled with creatures and the accidents of his brain." Within a week, plans were afoot for a collected edition of his works, to be edited by the Rev. Rufus Griswold.

Poe's anthologist, in fact, was none other than the author of that friendless *Herald* obituary. Yet he had, by some accounts, been handpicked by Poe himself. The choice was hardly surprising: with his 1842 *Poets and Poetry of America,* and the 1845 volume *Prose Writers of America,* Griswold was one of America's most influential anthologists. He'd known Poe for nearly a decade, to mixed results; though Poe described Griswold as "a gentleman of fine taste and sound judgment" in 1841, and he'd praised Poe as "highly imaginative" and "eminently distinguished," they'd also mortally offended each other at times. It hardly helped that, after Poe left *Burton's Gentleman's Magazine* in 1842, Griswold had taken his place. But the two reached a wary truce born of pragmatism, and Griswold's appreciation of Poe's talent was tangible: he'd given Edgar more space in an article on "Tale Writers" than to Cooper, Hawthorne, or even Washington Irving. For Poe, leaving his collected works in Griswold's hands was personally awkward, but a canny business decision.

"Poe was not my friend—I was not his—and he had no right to devolve upon me this duty of editing his works," Griswold complained to James Russell Lowell later that month. "He did so, however, and under the circumstances I could not well refuse compliance with the wishes of his friends here."

Griswold worked swiftly: along with collecting reminiscences by Poe's contemporaries Lowell and N. P. Willis, he placed newspaper ads to put out a call for copies of manuscripts and correspondence with Poe. Lost and unpublished work quickly turned up: Griswold's copy of Poe's final poem, "Annabel Lee," immediately appeared in print, while the Poe household's sometime nurse, Marie Shew, proved to have inspired the posthumously published poem "The Bells." Its hypnotically repetitive lines of "From the bells, bells, bells, bells . . ." would soon join "The Raven" as a public favorite. More letters, stories, poems, and marginalia poured in; scarcely three weeks after Poe died, six clerks were already at work setting copy for the New York publisher J. S. Redpath.

The Works of the Late Edgar Allan Poe, assembled at astonishing speed since his death on October 8, arrived in bookstores by January 10, 1850. Published into two green clothbound volumes—the first labeled *Tales,* and the second *Poems and Miscellanies*—they mark Poe's ascension into the canon of world literature. In life, Poe had never maintained a relationship with any one magazine, genre, or publisher long enough to build up a consistent audience; it is conceivable that no one admirer or critic had ever seen a majority of his complete writings. James Russell Lowell's comment on Poe's criticism applied just as readily to the rest of his work: "He has squared out blocks enough to build an enduring pyramid, but has left them lying carelessly and unclaimed in many different quarries."

Gathered together into two volumes totaling a thousand pages, the breadth of his accomplishments at last became apparent. Yet Griswold's personal criticisms of Poe left George Graham — who had employed both men as editors — fuming in print that Griswold "was not Mr. Poe's peer," and that his focus on Poe's poverty and drinking "looks so much like a breach of trust." Graham would find more to dislike when Griswold edited a third volume with Poe's criticism and "literati" sketches later that year; its biographical preface repeated many of the worst accusations against the man, whether true or not — claiming that Poe had been expelled from UVA, that he had been subject to "brutish drunkenness," that he contracted debts he could not pay.

"To think of that *villain* Griswold dragging before the public all my poor poor Eddie's *faults*," an outraged Maria Clemm wrote, "and not to have the generosity of speaking one word of his *good qualities*. . . . did you ever feel as if you wished *to die?* as if you wished to shut out the world and all that concerns it? *It is thus I feel.*"

Much of Griswold's biography was unobjectionable; many of its inaccuracies came from Poe's own tall tales. But in tiresomely emphasizing Poe's flaws through his correspondence, Griswold also engaged in a secret campaign of slander. So subtly as to even escape Aunt Maria's detection, he'd rewritten Poe's letters, inserting both base ingratitude and the occasional fawning praise of Griswold himself. "You so perfectly understand me," he has Poe enthuse: " . . . I can truly say no man's approbation gives me so much pleasure." It took the better part of a century to scrub Griswold's rather pathetic defacements from Poe's correspondence.

Yet Griswold's worst transgression against Poe's family was

a contractual one. There is no record of Poe having left a will; if he died intestate, his estate should have descended to his sister, Rosalie. Instead, it was Aunt Maria who negotiated away Poe's rights to Griswold — and scarcely even received anything in return. Though the books included a note from her thanking Griswold for publishing the books "for my benefit," Maria Clemm was only paid in copies, which poverty compelled her to sell. One of the first people to step up to help her out was Henry Wadsworth Longfellow — the very poet who was so often the target of both Poe's admiration and bewildering vitriol.

Longfellow understood Poe quite well, though. As a Harvard professor of poetry and linguistics who lived comfortably and was respected by the literary establishment — who had, in short, the life that Poe longed for — he intuited Poe's envy just as well as he understood his genius. Unlike Griswold, he had long forgiven it: "The harshness of his criticisms," Longfellow wrote, "I have never attributed to anything but the irritation of a sensitive nature, chafed by some indefinite sense of wrong."

Griswold, alas, was not so kind. And yet for all his betrayals of Poe's life, his editing of Poe's *art* was perfectly serviceable for the era — so much so that one might say that Poe's wisdom in entrusting his fame to him proved entirely justified. Even J. M. Daniel, a critic so hard on Poe that they'd once nearly dueled, was moved to this prophesy after reading the *Works:* "While people of this day run after such authors as Prescott and Willis . . . their children, in referring back to literary history, will say, 'This was the time of Poe.'"

The common notion is that Poe's name was blackened for generations after his death; it is one any publisher will find amusing, given the sale of tens of thousands of copies of *Works* during that time. Poe's personal failings, both real and imagined, probably had as little effect on his readership as it had on his heroes Byron and Coleridge. By 1860, he was so entirely embraced by the American public that a weekly "Raven Club" literary salon was held in Washington, D.C., by various senators and judges; even President Buchanan showed up for one meeting. Not to be outdone, Lincoln's presidential campaign biography that year boasted that he read three authors for pleasure: Robert Burns, William Shakespeare, and Edgar Allan Poe. In particular, Abe was "pleased with the absolute and logical method of Poe's tales and sketches, in which the problem of the mystery is given, and wrought out into everyday facts by processes of cunning analysis. It is said that he suffers no year to pass without the perusal of this author."

It is a telling commentary on how authors control what they write, but not what is read. Poe regarded his tales of ratiocination as something of a distraction; his great loves were poetry and his "prose poem," *Eureka*. "The Raven" was indeed Poe's most famous work during his lifetime, and time has not lessened its charms — but as art it is distinctly backward-looking. Poets still find kinship in Walt Whitman and Emily Dickinson, but one would be hard-pressed to find many who claim Poe as a profound influence. It is a mastery of narrative voice — and above all, the creation of the detective story — that made Poe an author that Lincoln and the world at large placed beside Shakespeare.

Yet it was indeed a fellow poet, Charles Baudelaire, who would prove Poe's greatest advocate abroad. After first coming across his work in France in 1847, Baudelaire felt that he had discovered the work of a blood brother. "I felt a singular excitement," he later explained. " . . . I found poems and stories which I had thought about, but in a vague, confused, and disordered way, and about which Poe had been able to treat perfectly. . . . The first time I opened one of his books I saw, to my amazement and delight, not only certain subjects which I had dreamed of, but *sentences* which I had thought out, written by him twenty years before."

Poe could well be called the adopted son of France. Through Baudelaire's tireless volumes of translation in the 1850s and 1860s, Poe's poetic creed of beauty for its own sake spoke to a rising generation of bohemians and Decadent poets; his science fiction deeply moved Jules Verne, who wrote his novel *The Sphinx of the Ice Fields* as a continuation of *The Narrative of Arthur Gordon Pym,* and dedicated it to Poe. It was also Baudelaire's edition that reached Fyodor Dostoevsky, who wrote the introduction to the 1861 Russian edition of Poe's works, just as he was on the cusp of creating his own masterpiece of tortured narration in *Notes from Underground.*

The most peculiarly ardent audience for Poe's work, though, would also prove to be its most influential. "The character and works of Poe have ever been held in reverence by the metaphysical minds of the Scottish universities," reported one newspaper in 1875. It was the fall of that year that the University of Edinburgh enrolled a young Arthur Conan Doyle. In Poe's tales of Dupin, the medical student found the artistic catalyst for his training in physical observation and diagnosis. The result was one of the great literary creations of his time: Sherlock Holmes.

"If every man who wrote a story which was indirectly inspired by Poe were to pay a tithe towards a monument," Doyle later mused, "it would be such as would dwarf the pyramids."

In fact, a more modest campaign to Poe's memory was coming to pass in the autumn of 1875. Rumors circulated for years that Poe was left in a potter's field, and in 1860 his aunt Maria wrote to Poe's Baltimore cousin Neilson Poe after hearing even worse: "A lady called on me a short time ago from Baltimore. She said she had visited my darling Eddie's grave. She said it was in the basement of the church, covered with rubbish and coal.

Is this true?" It wasn't, but Dr. Snodgrass, who'd tried in vain to save Poe in his final days, grimly scolded in 1856 that the truth was "bad, and discreditable enough to his relatives, not to say the city in which he died." A new church had already been built over much of the graveyard, and he warned that Poe's lonely grave might indeed soon be lost: "It is quite probable that the bones of 'Poor Poe' will be collected among the remains of the friendless and the unknown, and removed beyond recognition, for nothing but a couple of pine boards were placed at his grave, in lieu of a tombstone."

Fate itself even seemed to intervene: when Neilson Poe finally ordered a headstone, a locomotive crashed into the stonemason's studio and dashed it to pieces. And then, with the Civil War about to begin, that and a great many other plans rather went to the wayside. By the time that Aunt Maria died in 1871, and was buried next to Poe, his grave still remained unmarked. In the end, the rescue of America's dark and romantic poet would have to come from — schoolmistresses.

"They are to hold a meeting and arrange a literary entertainment," reported the *Baltimore Sun* in 1865, on the "schoolma'ams" working to buy "a suitable monument in this city to the memory of the late Edgar A. Poe."

A decade of collected pennies, appeals to patrons, and gamely staged fundraisers later, they had their marble monument. A prominent spot in the graveyard presented itself as a resting place for both Poe and his aunt Maria, but that meant their bodies had to be moved. The sexton was an old hand in such matters, having also buried Poe the first time around. But the cheap coffin hadn't stood up well; as the dirt was cleared away, the top corner collapsed, and its occupant indulgently gave his public one last ghastly fright: "Nothing remained inside the coffin but the skeleton," reported the local newspaper — before adding, in a touch worthy of Poe, that "some hair yet attached to the skull, and the teeth, which appeared all white and perfect, were shaken out of the jaws and lay at the bottom of the coffin."

He was gently moved into the new plot, and his monument unveiled on a chilly November day in 1875. A school holiday was called in the city, and over a thousand Baltimoreans spilled out of an assembly hall near the graveyard; spectators crowded onto porches and leaned out of the windows of surrounding houses. Along with Baltimore's schoolteachers, a tall and gray-bearded eminence could also be spotted in the crowd — Walt Whitman, now some three decades from the brash young Brooklyn printer whom Poe had published in the *Broadway Journal.* Joining him were those in whom the living memory of Poe still survived: his cousin Neilson, his old schoolmate Joe Clarke, and John Latrobe — one of the judges in the *Saturday Visiter* contest that had given Poe his first real break in 1833.

The man Latrobe recalled in his speech was not the gloomy poet of legend, but a hard-working and imaginative craftsman: meeting Edgar for the first time, he'd found the young man busy planning his "Hans Pfaall" lunar hoax, and eager to explain the conceit of a shoemaker flying to the moon in a balloon. "He ascended higher and higher, until, at last, he reached the point in space where the moon's attraction overcame that of the earth," the old editor mused over Poe's explanation of the passenger compartment suddenly flipping over. "The speaker had become so excited, spoke so excitedly, gesticulating much, that when the turn-upside-down took place, and he clapped his hands and stamped his foot by way of emphasis, I was carried along with him . . . he apologized for his excitability, which he laughed at himself."

The assembly proceeded to the new grave that would come to serve as a burial place for Edgar, Virginia, and Aunt Maria, reuniting the peculiar household that been Poe's sorrow and solace in life. There they read aloud his final poem, "Annabel Lee"— and in its last lines, the farewell of an artist finally at rest:

> *And so, all the night-tide, I lie down by the side*
> *Of my darling — my darling — my life and my bride*
> *In her sepulchre there by the sea —*
> *In her tomb by the sounding sea.*

Notes

As this is a brief biography, I will spare readers reference to facts already commonly covered in standard works of Poe scholarship (see the appendix of "Selected Further Readings"). However, for material that is unusual or even unique to this volume, I note the sources below.

1. The Child of Fortune (1809–1827)

Among numerous examples of advertisements for theatrical benefits for the Poes, see *The Repertory* (Boston) for September 18, 1807; March 11, 1808; and March 18, 1808; and *The Democrat* (Boston) for February 3, 1808; April 20, 1808; March 4, 1809; and April 19, 1809. Examples of benefits for three other colleagues can be seen in the *Boston Mirror* for March 11, 1809; April 15, 1809; and April 29, 1809.

An example of Ellis & Allan's wares can be seen in their *Richmond Enquirer* ad of October 18, 1811; the Manhattan that the Allans returned to from abroad can be glimpsed in that day's *New York Commercial Advertiser* of July 2, 1820. Numerous examples of academy ads are in the *Richmond Enquirer* of December 27, 1826.

William Mavor's *The English Spelling Book* (1803) is quoted regarding Poe's textbooks, and the example of "capping" comes from "Capping Verses" in *The Living Age* (October 1886).

Rev. Bransby's recollection of Poe may be found in William Elijah Hunter's *Athenaeum* article "Poe and His English Schoolmaster" (October 19, 1878). Numerous biographies quote Poe's "William Wilson" in describing Bransby's school, yet Hunter makes it clear that "the Dr. Bransby of the tale, with the exception of his name, is quite as much a product of Poe's imagination as is the schoolhouse itself."

2. Manuscript Found in a Bottle (1827–1838)

Although accounts of Poe considering joining the Greek revolution have always been regarded as rather fanciful, the *Essex Register* of May 28, 1827, does indeed note that a Greek Committee in Boston was about to send volunteers and supplies to the conflict.

To my knowledge, the possibility of "A Fragment" being by Edgar has not been previously noted in Poe scholarship. Edgar and Henry Poe's writings in the short-lived *North American* magazine of 1827 certainly remain a tantalizingly obscure area of study, not least because of the scarcity of the publication itself. The issues noted in this chapter contain "The Happiest Day" (September 15, 1827), "Dreams" (October 20, 1827), and "A Fragment" (November 3, 1827), and can be found on microfilm. The one book on the subject is itself now old and uncommon, but Hervey Allen's *Poe's Brother: The Poems of William Henry Leonard Poe* (1926) remains useful, particularly as it includes plates reproducing the articles.

Scandalized readers needing reassurance of the legality of Poe's peculiar marriage may find it in pages 398–400 of *The Revised Code of the Laws of Virginia* (1819).

3. The Glorious Prospect (1838–1844)

The rising interest in puzzles by periodicals during Poe's time has never received its scholarly due; still, a sense of the genre at the time can be gleaned from such collections as *The London Riddler; Or, the Arts of Teasing Made Easy* (1830), and by looking back to such predecessors as Jonathan Puzzle's *The Labyrinth* (1753). A number of Poe's cryptograms and other puzzles were gathered by Clarence S. Brigham in *Edgar Allan Poe's Contributions to Alexander's Weekly Messenger* (1943); they can be readily found today on the eapoe.org website.

One of Poe's ciphers—from his final puzzle column at *Graham's Magazine,* which he claimed he couldn't be bothered to run the solution to—went unsolved until 2000, when the Toronto software engineer Gil Broza cracked it. Deciphered, and bedevilled by some printing errors in the original, it proved to be a pun on sun/son and air/heir:

It was early spring, warm and sultry glowed the afternoon. The very breezes seemed to share the delicious languor of universal nature, are laden the various and mingled perfumes of the rose and the -essaerne, the woodbine and its wildflower. They slowly wafted their fragrant offering to the open window where sat the lovers. The ardent sun shoot fell upon her blushing face and its gentle beauty was more like the creation of romance or the fair inspiration of a dream than the actual reality on earth. Tenderly her lover gazed upon her as the clusterous ringlets were edged by amorous and sportive zephyrs and when he perceived the rude intrusion of the sunlight he sprang to draw the curtain but softly she stayed him. "No, no, dear Charles," she softly said, "much rather you'ld [sic] I have a little sun than no air at all."

Though some wondered whether Poe wrote the source text, I find that it previously appeared in the *Baltimore Sun* of July 4, 1840; and that it was in turn based on a widely reprinted poem ("Nuptial Repartee") that first appeared in the June 21, 1813, *Morning Herald* of London. A manuscript in the hand of Hester Thrale (i.e., Hester Lynch Piozzi) in Harvard's library hints that she may be the true author.

As for the gym Poe visited, the story of its colorful owner Samuel Barrett might be lost to history altogether were it not for an account within the obituary of his wife, Mary Barrett; it can be found in the *Daily Picayune* (New Orleans) for January 18, 1888.

James Curtis's *The Murder of Maria Marten* (1827) is explored further in my November 2006 article for *The Believer*, "The Molecatcher's Daughter"; Patricia Cline Cohen details the role of the *New York Herald* and James Gordon Bennett in her 1999 study *The Murder of Helen Jewett*.

An account of claims by Captain Kidd's would-be sister ran in the *Times-Picayune* (New Orleans) on August 4, 1842; the amusingly opportunistic ad for the "Gold Bug" lottery appears in the *Baltimore Sun* for August 14, 1843.

4. The Shakespeare of America (1844–1847)

Life in the city is summarized at the start of the chapter through the April 6, 1844, issue of the *New York Tribune;* the slower pace of life in Fordham can be

gathered from the *Herald* headline from October 20, 1844, GREAT PLOUGH-
ING AND SPADING MATCH AT FORDHAM.

Examples of newspaper stories on transatlantic ballooning that ran before
Poe's hoax can be found in the *New York Commercial Advertiser* of February 8,
1800, the *Southern Patriot* (Charleston, SC) of May 12, 1825, and the *Baltimore
Sun* for January 10, 1840; May 4, 1840; and June 15, 1843.

The "discovery" and subsequent fraud allegations around Captain Kidd's
treasure can be found in the *Brooklyn Eagle* for July 2, 1844; July 5, 1844; and
January 3, 1848; it can also be read of in "The Kidd Humbug — Its Explosion"
in the *Southern Patriot* (Charleston, SC) for July 22, 1847. The *Evening Mirror*
(New York) item for January 8, 1845, on the venture may have been written by
Poe himself — and as an editor there, if he didn't write about the Kidd hunters,
he certainly knew of them.

Poe's stint at writing a campaign song is recalled in the *Brooklyn Daily
Eagle* of November 17, 1875, and in "Edgar Allan Poe: Reminiscences of Ga-
briel Harrison, an Actor, Still Living in Brooklyn" in *The Book Lover* (Vol. 1,
Winter 1899–1900).

Maria Clemm's overdue back taxes are revealed in a published notice in
the *Baltimore Sun* of January 9, 1846, while the *New York Tribune* of February
14, 1846, carried news of the extra letter carriers hired for Valentine's Day. The
work among Fourier colonies by Mrs. Gove can be seen in the March 15, 1845,
issue of the *Weekly Herald* (New York).

5. Nevermore (1848–1875)

Both Poe's lecture advertising and a sense of his competition can be gathered
from the *New York Herald* for February 2, 3, and 4, 1848; the *Evening Express*
of February 4, 1848, and the *New York Tribune* of February 3 and 8, 1848, also
contain useful information.

The weather on the weekend of Poe's discovery is from the *Baltimore Sun*
of October 4, 1849. While a number of newspapers wondered about Poe's remains in the years after his death, the example cited in this chapter is from
Trenton State Gazette of September 12, 1854, and Dr. Snodgrass's complaints
were reprinted in the *Weekly Wisconsin Patriot* of June 28, 1856.

The cause of Poe's death remains famously disputed, though at the time
it was universally (and quite reasonably) attributed to alcohol. "Why not ac-

knowledge the truth?" asked the New York *Weekly Herald* on October 20, 1849. "Hard drinking is the besetting sin of our fine poets and romancers."

Details of the Raven Club can be gleaned from the City Intelligence sections of *The Constitution* (Washington, D.C.) of February 4, 1860, and December 8, 1860.

Among the various calls for a monument to Poe, the earliest appearance of the campaign by Baltimore schoolteachers is in the *Baltimore Sun* of November 7, 1865; its unveiling is covered a decade later in a lengthy front-page story in that same paper, on November 18, 1875. This account includes such details as the attendance of one thousand spectators, as well as the declaration of a school holiday. The ceremony is also covered in *Edgar A. Poe: A Memorial Volume* (1877), which is reproduced at the eapoe.org website.

Although it would take years to finish the task, the notion of moving his wife Virginia's remains was already being mulled by the time of the ceremony, as is shown by articles in the *Baltimore Sun* on October 8, 1875, and October 11, 1875.

Doyle's remark on the debt that detective writers owe to Poe was published in the *New York Times* article "Honor Poe in London" on March 2, 1909; it remains just as true today.

Selected Further Reading

Primary Documents

The Poe Log, ed. Dwight Thomas and David K. Jackson (G. K. Hall & Co., 1987).

> Clearly a labor of love, this chronological montage of letters, journal entries, and newspaper clippings models itself to great effect after Jay Leyda's *The Melville Log* (1951). Although necessarily selective, this documentary approach conveys the breadth of Poe's life and interest better than most erstwhile biographies — it is a reference work that doubles as a very illuminating narrative on Poe. The entire text has been helpfully included on the eapoe.org website.

The Collected Letters of Edgar Allan Poe (3rd edition), ed. John Ward Ostrom et al. (Gordian Press, 2008).

> A key resource in Poe scholarship, this is the most recent expansion and revision of previous 1948 and 1966 editions of Poe's collected letters. Earlier collections of Poe's correspondence are not as trustworthy, particularly given the baleful influence of Griswold's forgeries.

Collected Editions of Poe

UNIVERSITY OF ILLINOIS PRESS EDITIONS
Complete Poems. Ed. Thomas Mabbott (2000).
Tales & Sketches, Vol. 1: 1831–1842. Ed. Thomas Mabbott (2000).
Tales & Sketches, Vol. 2: 1843–1849. Ed. Thomas Mabbott (2000).
Eureka. Ed. Stuart Levine and Susan F. Levine (2004).
Critical Theory: The Major Documents. Ed. Stuart Levine and Susan F. Levine (2008).

Though the reprinted Mabbott volumes call out for a modern update, these annotated editions are the best scholarly editions for the close study of Poe.

Edgar Allan Poe: Poetry and Tales (The Library of America, 1984).
Edgar Allan Poe: Essays and Reviews (The Library of America, 1984).
Sturdy editions that capture the full range of Poe's works, the ready availability of these volumes makes them useful for graduate-level work.

Edgar Allan Poe: Complete Tales and Poems (Vintage Books, 1975).
Cramped, cheap, and nearly complete: its art-nouveau cover has been a campus icon for generations, and with good reason. This edition remains the classic undergrad text to this day.

The Portable Edgar Allan Poe, ed. Gerald Kennedy. (Penguin Books, 2006).
A thematically arranged selection of Poe's best-known works. While it can't quite convey his range and idiosyncrasies, it's a handy annotated edition of his classics.

Biographies

Edgar Allan Poe: A Critical Biography. Arthur Hobson Quinn (Johns Hopkins University Press, 1941, 1998 rpt.).
Seven decades on, this remains the greatest and most complete of Poe biographies. Quinn is unafraid to quote — and to quote often — from documents for pages at a time, sometimes acting less as an interpreter than as a well-informed guide through a Poe archive. While correcting Griswold's depredations loomed larger in 1941 than it needs to today, Quinn's work remains largely unsurpassed.

Edgar A. Poe: Mournful and Never-ending Remembrance. Kenneth Silverman (HarperCollins, 1991).
The best modern biography on Poe, despite its insistence on pathologizing his life. Silverman's contextual detail is excellent; he takes pains, for

instance, to dig up just what Poe's daily routine in the Army would have been. When the psychoanalysis is given a rest, Silverman can be a fine and subtle interpreter of Poe's work.

Edgar Allan Poe: His Life and Legacy. Jeffrey Meyers (Charles Scribner's Sons, 1992).

Meyer's mid-length biography is well-rounded and approachable. Some of his assertions are stated with more certainty than the sources warrant; still, for readers looking to deepen their interest in Poe, his work is a good next step.

Acknowledgments

My books could not happen without the inspiration of my sons, Bramwell and Morgan, or without the love of my wife, Jennifer, who is the first reader of all that I write.

Marc Thomas valiantly held down the fort while I was off contemplating 1840s newspapers. My many thanks also go to my agent, Michelle Tessler, and my editor, James Atlas — and a tip of the stovepipe hat to Ed Park for getting me started.

I remain as indebted as ever to many libraries, including Portland State University, the New York Public Library, and the Library of Congress. My particular thanks also go to the Edgar Allan Poe Society of Baltimore (eapoe.org), whose devotion to placing Poe scholarship online makes its website an invaluable resource for readers.

Index